Richard Oostra's involvement in Christian ministry leadership over a period of more than fifty years, throughout North America as well as on the Continent, has enabled him to have a unique perspective on the state of the church as it has evolved into its current condition. His analysis of the distressing conditions and serious shortcomings generally evident in the church today is most insightful and urgently needs to be carefully considered. More importantly, his call for repentance and corrective action is one that we fail to heed to our peril and to serious loss for the cause of Christ.

Dr. William R. Goetz
author and long-term pastor and administrator

As a layman in the pew, the author is expressing his frustration between belief and total commitment in aspect of both church life and one's personal life to a Christ who has done so much for us.

Whether agreeing or not with the author's premises, one cannot escape the fact that *Church on the Rocks* is a clarion call to the church to take a hard look at what it is truly all about anyway. It will provoke our thinking in many different aspects of church-life today. Whatever your thoughts, let the heartbeat of the author stir you to action in some areas of your life.

Rev. Lou Sutera, Evangelist
Canadian Revival Fellowship

Richard Oostra has been a personal friend of mine for eighteen years. He is a person who loves the Lord and His church. While here his influence was strong in the areas of evangelism and grounding new Christians in the Word of God. His criticisms may startle you, but his interest is to see the church built on a sound scriptural foundation. He is a man that has a great heart for the church.

James W. Sinclair, Pastor (1969-1987)
Bethany Baptist Church, Red Deer, AB

This book makes it very clear that the church is in need of another reformation. She has never been fully restored of being a deteriorating system. She needs to become again that dynamic and mysterious organism the early church has been.

Rev. M.J.

Church on the Rocks

CHURCH ON THE ROCKS

Richard Oostra

forever books
WINNIPEG, CANADA
www.foreverbooks.ca

Cover Design: Yvonne Parks Design
Book Design: Andrew Mackay
Managing Editor: Beryl Henne

Contact: Richard Oostra
P.O. Box 2667
Blaine WA 98231
www.RichardOostra.com

All Royalties from this project are given to the: Mennonite Foundation of Canada

Forever Books

WINNIPEG CANADA

www.foreverbooks.ca

Warning

If you are satisfied with today's church, then this book may not be for you.

If you struggle with concerns about the visible church in the early twenty-first century, you may be encouraged to know you are not alone.

Within these pages, you will find a look at where the present-day church is failing. More importantly, you will discover a simple summary of our Lord's Divine Blueprint for the church that He founded, as well as biblical suggestions on how to live as He intended in our critical and perplexing times.

Richard Oostra

Contents

Part Two: The Solution for the Church: *Changes That Urgently Need to be Made*

Part Three: Where Do We Go From Here?

Appendices

Preface

The concepts presented in *Church on the Rocks* have been developed and, in some cases, published over a period of many years as I became increasingly concerned about a number of conditions and changes I observed within evangelical and other churches throughout North America.

My intent has never been to undermine the church. I love the church. Writing the material in this book has not been a pleasant task. Unfortunately, some have felt I am anti-church, which has made for my personal unpopularity in some quarters.

Nevertheless, at the urging of some of those who read these writings, I have recently collected them into a manuscript I circulated to a number of Christian pastors and leaders whom I respected in the Lord. I asked them to mercilessly critique them.

The responses both encouraged and disheartened me. The encouragement came from the fact that there was a high degree of agreement by the reviewers with the basic thrust of what I had written. Most felt the message urgently needed to be said, despite the likelihood that it would not be popular with the church in general and that as a layman with no axe to grind, I could state these unpopular truths more easily than could a pastor or other church leader.

The discouragement came from the frequently expressed comment that there was far too much repetition in the manuscript and it needed to be severely edited—something that I did not feel qualified to do. Nevertheless, I agreed with the accuracy of the assessments, recognizing that the manuscript was basically a collection of material produced over a long period of time.

A fairly extensive critique was done by an author of several best-selling books. I soon felt in my spirit that the writer of the critique was the person who could and should put the manuscript into the proper shape. After a good deal of discussion and a lengthy period of prayerful consideration, he agreed to do so under the pen name of Wilhelm G. Ralph. The book you hold in your hands is the result of our collaboration.

Our prayer is that the Lord may use these thoughts to stimulate, encourage, and motivate you to be a catalyst for whatever God wants to do through you for His glory in the church that He intended.

Richard Oostra

Introduction

The enormous and rapid changes that have marked almost every aspect of our culture in recent years have also been felt within the church at large. As a result, the traditional church of yesteryear has, in fact, virtually disappeared.

Always, of course, our Lord preserves for Himself a faithful remnant, and we recognize that here and there remain faithful, God-honoring churches in which the Word of God is carefully taught, the Lord Jesus Christ is exalted, and believers are growing in their walk with Him, their use of spiritual gifts and their fruit-bearing. This book is not about those churches. They are to be commended, and the use of the term "Today's church" should not be construed either to include them or as a failure to recognize their faithful service. Yet it remains true that the traditional church of yesteryear has largely disappeared from today's church scene.

This, in itself, is not entirely bad, since admittedly there were many shortcomings in various aspects of yesterday's church. Nevertheless, what has taken the place of that traditional church has created many legitimate and extremely disturbing concerns in the hearts and minds of numerous Christians. The pervasive and growing influence of what is called "the emergent church"—

though to a large degree under the radar of most Christians—has added immeasurably to this concern.

Consequently it is not unusual to see articles such as "How Do I Find a Good Church?" by Hank Hanegraaff of The Christian Research Institute, or a pastoral letter from "Grace to You" Bible teacher Dr. John MacArthur in which he indicates that he is often asked to describe the non-negotiables to be considered when someone is searching for, or evaluating, a church.

This volume addresses the same issue by taking a look at the state of the visible church, generally, in North America today, and then contrasting it with the church that the founder, the Lord Jesus Christ, intended—as revealed in the Divine Blueprint, the Word of God.

The doctrines, structure, practices, membership, and ministry of the contemporary church, as well as the biblical directives on the same issues, will be considered in the context of one of the scriptural pictures of the Church—a building of God.

Quotations of Scripture used throughout the book are mostly taken from the King James Version and New International Version of the Holy Bible.

PART ONE:

The State of the Church

Section A

Essential Characteristics in Waning Evidence in Today's Church

I love the church.

Consequently, I have found little pleasure in writing about my concerns over the serious lack of the essential characteristics of a biblically healthy church that I have observed in many of North America's churches.

The list is not exhaustive nor is it in any particular order of priority. The following are some of the characteristics that I perceive to be generally lacking in today's church.

May our recognition and acknowledgement of these circumstances lead to genuine repentance and a return to biblical ministries.

Biblical Preaching

The apostle Paul admonished,
Preach the word; be ready in season and out of season;
reprove, rebuke, exhort.

2 Timothy 4:2 NASB

All Scripture is inspired by God and profitable for
teaching, for reproof, for correction, for training in
righteousness; so that the man of God may be adequate,
equipped for every good work.

(2 Timothy 3:16–17 NASB)

The church today is in desperate need of pastors who are
prophets as well as laypeople who will dare to speak up for biblical
truth and lead the church into restoration. We need to be open to
truth from the Word of God, and when we see it, we must walk in it.

David Wilkerson recently wrote that he knows of many preachers who receive a salary but do not minister for the Lord. They have no burden from Him. They don't seek God diligently in prayer. They don't get their sermons from Him and from His Word. Instead, they borrow their messages from others. Such ministers, Wilkerson said, are merely hirelings, getting a check for simply doing a job. They are prayer-less, with no fresh word from heaven.

Wilkerson also mentions the fact that it sadly is often the case that laypeople have a much deeper knowledge of Christ and the Word than the men who pastor them. Such are intercessors, hungry for truth, serving God wholeheartedly. They are given to prayer, shutting themselves in with Christ. These, he says, are true ministers, having outgrown their pastors long ago. These, like Isaiah or Jeremiah, will be used by God to lead the church into restoration and repentance.

Today's "profession of ministry" involves more than merely getting paid for ministry. The approach used for employing clergy largely does away with the concept of sacrificial servanthood given to proclaiming God's Word. It tends to follow commercial practices, with substantial compensation and responsibilities that emphasize church administration, similar to the role of a chief executive officer.

This approach, which is no longer based upon God's Word, will inevitably lead to more church divisions and departures because it has within it the seeds of decay. The apostle Paul wrote clearly to the Corinthian believers:

"If the trumpet does not sound a clear call, who will get ready for battle?" (1 Corinthians 14:8).

It is *the Word of God* that must be the directive in the supernatural functioning and operation of the church. It is Christ who by His Spirit wants to be the unseen director in the church for whom He died and rose again. Many churches are not formed by Christ's design nor controlled by the Spirit, but by cleverly formulated methods of men.

20

THE WORD OF GOD IS AUTHORITATIVE

For the early church, the Word of God was the prophetically spoken word. For us it can also be spoken, but it must always be in line with the revealed written Word of God. When sermons are based on men's ideas, human philosophies, or unbiblical interpretations of God's Word, the Holy Spirit is grieved and the church is in trouble.

The Bible teaches that God's Word is truth (John 17:17). Hearing comes by the Word (Romans 10:17). Obedience must be to God's Word (Psalm 119:9), and God's Word never changes (Matthew 24:35).

With Martin Luther, church leaders must learn to say, "My conscience is held captive by *the Word of God*" (emphasis added). It is to the Word of God we must turn, and to that Word I endeavor to be true in the following pages.

COMMITTED TO THE WORD OR MEN PLEASERS?

Many pastors are denomination or congregation pleasers. They are delivering the "kind words" and "soft strokes" that people are looking for rather than the pure Word of the Lord. The multiple ministries of the Holy Spirit that Jesus designed for the church are considered "not for today." Let us listen to the prophets of old:

> *My people have been lost sheep; their shepherds have led them astray and caused them to roam on the mountains ... Whoever found them devoured them.*
>
> (Jeremiah 50:6–7)

These slothful and even false shepherds have entered the pulpit in many churches. They no longer preach the Word primarily but rather tell stories and use unbiblical methods to maintain the church as well as their careers. *Expository preaching of the Word of God is gone* from most pulpits, and there is a great famine in the land. The Lord says:

> *I am against the shepherds and will hold them accountable for my flock. I will remove them from tending the flock so that the shepherds can no longer feed themselves.*
>
> (Ezekiel 34:10)

Most believers today can be characterized as part of an *illiterate generation in terms of Bible knowledge.* Our youth have become easy prey for atheistic university professors while many adults are turning to TV evangelists. The church of today, through *failure to preach and teach God's Word,* has left believers open to large scale deception and as prey for the antichrist, when he will appear with great signs and wonders.

The apostle Peter, when speaking about the end-times, wrote:

> *There will be false teachers among you. They will secretly introduce destructive heresies, even denying the sovereign Lord ... Many will follow their shameful ways ... In their greed these teachers will exploit you with stories they have made up.*
>
> (2 Peter 2:1–3)

The only safeguard we have against destructive heresies is a *thorough knowledge of the Word of God.* We must turn to the Word of God and to shepherds who preach the Word and have the prophetic message of repentance and sanctification for the people of the church. Tragically, sound biblical preaching is no longer heard in many, or perhaps even most, of the churches of our day.

Exaltation of the Lord Jesus Christ

Christ loved the church and gave himself up for her to make her holy, cleansing her by the washing with water through the word, and to present her to himself as a radiant church, without stain or wrinkle or any other blemish, but holy and blameless.

Ephesians 5:25–27

Are our lives being controlled by men or directed by God? The early Christians addressed Jesus as Savior and *Lord.* As our Lord, He demands to be the ruler and king in our lives as well as in the church. Here is what He said: *"Why do you call me 'Lord, Lord' and do not do what I say?"* (Luke 6:46). *"You are my friends if you do what I command"* (John 15:14). *"The sinful nature desires what is contrary to the Spirit ... those who live like this will not inherit the kingdom of God"* (Galatians 5:17, 21).

Jesus stated that *He* would build his Church; however, many churches now bear little of Christ's design, His headship, or His

23

presence. Like commercial institutions, they are earthly in design and of such we are told to beware.

If we, through the Spirit, live obedient lives we will demonstrate the kingship of Christ. His kingdom is where His will is being done, and for this we need the transforming resurrection power of Christ within us. Without Him, we can only perform in the flesh and are able to do absolutely nothing. He is the Vine and we are the branches. Because of this, the apostle Paul wrote:

> *I want to know Christ and the power of his resurrection and the fellowship of sharing in his sufferings, becoming like him in his death, and so, somehow, to attain to the resurrection from the dead ... Forgetting what is behind and straining toward what is ahead, I press on toward the goal to win the prize for which God has called me heavenward in Christ Jesus.*
>
> (Philippians 3:10–14)

> *I can do everything through him who gives me strength.*
>
> (Philippians 4:13)

This song by Judson W. Van DeVenter (1855–1939) says it so beautifully:

> *"All to Jesus I surrender,*
> *Lord, I give myself to Thee.*
> *Fill me with Thy love and power;*
> *Let Thy blessing fall on me."*

It is Christ who by His Spirit wants to be the unseen director in the church for which He died and rose again. Many churches are not formed by Christ's design nor controlled by His Spirit. Instead, they operate in accordance with cleverly formulated methods of men.

A major cause is the significant absence of the proclamation of the biblical call to yield to the Lordship of Christ. Instead, the major thrust from many pulpits—as well as in the literature and study materials—is aimed at how to find the "fulfilled" life that Christ suffered and died to provide. "Christianity" has become man-centered instead of Christ-centered.

Instead of being supernaturally designed and directed by Christ, today's church, in many places, is structured by human design; many Christians live in spiritual bondage to man-made edicts instead of living by the clear teaching of Scripture. Despite the Reformation and sporadic subsequent renewals, the spiritually-equipped ministries Christ meant us to use are largely being ignored.

Further, many of today's churches have imposed a myriad of rules, regulations, restrictions, and reservations that regulate the conduct of their members. Rather than welcoming newcomers into Christ's church based on our oneness in Christ, attention is often focused on adherence to narrow interpretations and church doctrine. Like the Pharisees of Jesus' day, they have no interest in or tolerance for other views. Perhaps even the apostle Paul would have trouble being accepted in many of today's churches.

Biblically speaking, the church local and universal:

- fully belongs to God, 1 Timothy 3:15.
- is founded by Christ, 1 Corinthians 3:11.
- has Christ as its Head, Ephesians 1:22.
- is made up of His followers, Acts 2:47.
- has ministers equipped and supplied by Him, Ephesians 4:11–12.

His teachings clearly show that Jesus sought to direct the church and have its members be Spirit-controlled. But, do most church members experience Christ's presence and power when they meet? Do they gather to hear from Him or just from men? Do they seek His presence or the "celebration" of a large crowd?

Jesus promised that as long as He was exalted to His rightful place as Head of the church, His Spirit would be in control. The Spirit would lead, teach, guide, and supply leadership and growth in the church (John 16:13). Today, most churches seem to have lost their dependence on the Spirit and have looked for artificial means of growth.

As church decline continues (both in attendance and commitment to biblical principles), because the Spirit's presence and direction is missing, leaders are turning to even more carnal methods to "save" the church. Instead of seeking renewal in accordance with the Scriptures (Jeremiah 7:3) and yielding to the lordship of Christ, they turn to human wisdom, thus revealing how dull their thinking has become. The Scripture says those who are without the Spirit cannot understand the things of God (1 Corinthians 2:14). So these churches continue to change:

- From singing proven hymns to reciting repetitive choruses
- From sharing Christ-centered music to performing music of the contemporary culture
- From the mindful worship of God to stirring up of the emotions
- From qualified elder control to corporate leadership
- From serving as a house of prayer to being a community gathering center
- From encouraging use of spiritual gifts to employing professionals
- From searching the Scriptures to pulpit indoctrination
- From proclaiming God's Word to spreading human philosophies
- From submitting to Christ's design to accepting corporate structure

These illustrations are a clear indication that the Lord Jesus Christ is not being exalted in the church that professes to own Him as its Head.

Involvement in Ministry by the Membership

He ... gave some to be pastors and teachers, to prepare
God's people for works of service.
Ephesians 4:11–12, emphasis added

People like to go to a church where there is life and enthusiasm, where people become involved in using their spiritual gifts to serve the Lord. There is nothing more disheartening than being limited merely to attending, listening, and supporting. A church ought to be a beehive of creative activity, in which reports of praise and thanksgiving for what God has been doing *in and through the members* of the body are continually heard.

Sometimes, where the pastoral role has become dominant, the church body has become inactive and stagnant. Believers go to church with a spectator attitude and leave completely unchallenged, unchanged, unmotivated, and uninvolved in ministry. Nor are they being prepared for ministry, as God's Word says they should be.

THE PASTORATE WAS NEVER MEANT TO BE A ONE-MAN MINISTRY

The Scripture supports the concept of a plurality of leadership. Even as Jethro advised Moses to delegate his work, pastoral ministry also needs to be a shared ministry (1 Corinthians 12:27–30). Ministries are most effective when operating in teams. The lack of this can easily lead to pastor burnout, an epidemic in the church today. Jesus and His apostles worked in teams. Not just the pastor (or pastors), not only the elder board, but the entire church is meant to be ministering. In fact, according to Ephesians, the biblical responsibility of pastors is to equip the flock for ministry.

PASTORS SHOULD SHARE THE PRIVILEGE OF LEADERSHIP

Pastoral ministry is just one of many ministries Christ has made available to his Church. Pastors need not base their organizational concept on maintaining control because of a fear of losing dominance. But this is a great danger. In fact one-man pastoring can easily lead a church astray. Messages should never come from a single messenger but should be compared with those of other prophets. Every message needs to conform to God's Word. Jesus continually offered His disciples opportunities to minister. The task of every leader is to multiply himself by developing other leaders. If other persons in a flock have developed the ability to lead, then the pastor should, in all humility, allow those persons to minister, for it is by helping others to succeed that ministry achieves success; the whole church will be blessed!

Jesus intended that His church comprise a holy priesthood who would continue His work. He did not intend it to be a mixed gathering of spectators who merely come and listen to a lecture once a week from a speaker who seeks to interpret the Bible as he or his leadership sees it with no discussion from others—even those who may have a clearer understanding. Most churches, however, leave the work of the ministry up to a few people. This is the way most churches operate. These people, being good employees, try to organize the "church" toward bringing in more people, which hopefully means more funds and a grander image for the church.

Another reason for the lack of spiritual maturity among today's believers is that we are biblically illiterate so that we cannot reach our fullness in Christ. By not functioning according to passages such as Ephesians chapter four, we have failed to accept Christ's gifts or responsibility for spiritual equipping. In so doing, we have failed to recognize and use the Spirit's gifts to every member of the church. Even after the Reformation and periodic renewals, the spiritual equipping ministries Christ meant for us to have in the church are still being largely ignored.

The purpose of the church was and is that we should minister to one another, not that we simply have one man minister to us. The church was not meant to be a gathering to hear a lecture, but an equipping event. The church was not meant to divide God's people into "clergy and laity," but to build all God's people up to achieve their greatest potential to perform ministries for God. God's purpose for the church was to glorify Him by continuing Christ's ministry through the lives of believers.

PARTICIPATION

When more and more people become voluntarily involved with the function and ministry of the church, funds become available to help the poor and needy. As they reach out to those in need and participate in other outreaches of the church, people will no longer settle for a comfortable pew or stained glass windows;

they will gladly meet even in a school or warehouse, where there is plenty of parking, low financial overhead, flexible usefulness and room to grow if necessary in order to be productive members of Christ's body.

A vital function of the church is outreach, both within and outside the community. God is honored when His kingdom grows and believers become more firmly established in the faith. It is in doing that we grow, not in warming a pew (James 1:22).

The New Testament Church was an explosive church. Believers went in every direction and ministries exploded out from their midst. Jesus warned us when He said beware of the hired hand (John 10:12). He even promised to divinely equip the church in its ministerial needs (Ephesians 4:11), so that there would be a continuous supply of believers to carry on ministries and meet various needs within each church. Bringing in outside professional ministers instead of developing our own has tended to stunt spiritual growth, because believers are not called to involvement and have become merely spectators. This is a major cause of spiritual decay, deadness, and "sick" churches.

MINISTRIES IN THE CHURCH

It was he who gave some to be apostles, some to be prophets, some to be evangelists, and some to be pastors and teachers, to prepare God's people for works of service, so that the body of Christ may be built up until we all reach unity in the faith and in the knowledge of the Son of God and become mature, attaining to the whole measure of the fullness of Christ.

(Ephesians 4:11–13)

Before Christ left the earth He promised His followers His Spirit. Among the resulting blessings to the church and its believers are these three:

First, we have the *gift* of the indwelling Spirit, which is regeneration (John 16:8–11), giving us new life.

Second, we are enabled with the *fruit* of the Spirit to live sanctified lives, by striving for godly character (Galatians 5:23).

Third, the ministry gifts of the Spirit enables us for the ministry of building up the church and for functioning together as Christ's body (Romans 12:6–8).

MINISTRIES OF THE SPIRIT

It would greatly enhance the ministry of the church if we would welcome all of the ministries the Spirit has made available. The early church exercised the ministries of Ephesians 4:11–16; Romans 12; and 1 Corinthians 12; today, many ignore these, claiming that they are not for this age. However, we must exercise wisdom and care to properly divide the Word of God (2 Timothy 2:15) and to believe and receive what God has for us. The ministry gifts the Spirit gives the Church are apostles, prophets, evangelists, pastors (shepherds), and teachers. These are for the building up of the body and the maturing of believers.

APOSTLES AND EVANGELISTS, THE CHURCH PLANTERS

After Jesus said that He would build His church in Matthew 16:18, He commanded us to send His message to the ends of the earth. The first ministry function that the New Testament Church immediately recognized was that of apostolic teams. The twelve apostles are considered to be the foundational building stones of the New Testament Church. They were those who had been with the Lord and were witnesses to His earthly ministry, but the Bible also speaks of others as apostles (or evangelists) of the church as those who went forth starting new churches and extending the kingdom of God.

They used their spiritual gifts to reach beyond the established church, often going where Jesus had not yet been preached. They started new churches and ordained elders to lead in these new churches. Today, we usually send out missionaries repeatedly to the same location, where we seek to establish our own name. We no longer seek to establish new works nor have we encouraged the use of those gifted to do so. Our financial disbursements clearly reveal that we are not as eager in sending out Christ's message as the New Testament Church was. In spite of this, the Lord is still using some missionaries to blaze new trails for His church with a special anointing, equipping, and abundant blessing.

MINISTERS OF RECONCILIATION

As believers, God expects all of us to be actively involved in ministry. He has given us the ministry of reconciliation (2 Corinthians 5:18) and a wide variety of opportunities to edify the body of Christ and help all believers come to a unity of faith, knowing the Lord by experience. A church is meant to be a bee-hive of these activities, with continuous efforts toward reconciling, maturing, and activating believers for the work of their priestly ministry.

"You are a chosen people ... that you may declare the praises of him who called you out of darkness into his wonderful light" (1 Peter 2:9).

Some religious leaders like to claim supernatural powers for themselves. The Bible, however, teaches that the Spirit is the supernatural One, and the body of every believer is the temple of the Holy Spirit. Everyone who has trusted Christ has received His Spirit (1 Corinthians 6:19–20). We are to use the gifts the Spirit has imparted to us to participate in ministry and to function together as a harmonious whole.

The weakness of our system is especially obvious in those churches who depend on "professional leadership" and experience a pastor being "called to another church" and leaving. The congregation then becomes like a group of orphans without a shepherd, desperately seeking to find another stranger whose direction they can follow.

ELDERS: MINISTRY OF SHEPHERDING

Another serious error in the church today is the failure to adhere to biblical requirements regarding the characteristics and functioning of elders. Elders were meant to be key safeguards to the church; God-fearing men, gifted and able to serve as leaders.

Timothy and Titus both gave us descriptions of eldership and were among the first to appoint elders in the new churches (Titus 1:5). When the apostles wrote letters or contacted the churches, they always addressed the elders (Acts 20:17). Elders in the Old Testament era as well as in the early church were carefully chosen and ordained for duty (Acts 14:23) and they functioned as long as they were able to serve.

Today, many churches have a different approach toward eldership. Elders are voted into office for a year or two, but if they speak out in opposition to the views of the hired leadership, their names will likely not come up again for nomination. The Bible makes it clear that the elders are the key to the leadership of ministries in the church. Prophets, teachers, evangelists as well as pastors—all these are given to equip the church and its members for ministry, not to establish them with control or higher authority in the church.

Ministers in the church always worked in teams. Having multiple leaders provides checks and balances; it is through this group that God speaks, leads, and appoints. Those checks and balances were put in place to prevent domineering, assure balance and adherence to biblical principles. If there were problems in the church, the correction was addressed to the elders (Acts 15:2). These people were prayerfully chosen and meant to be obeyed and respected by the church. The Bible says elders as church leaders should be:

Shepherds of God's flock ... serving ... not because you must, but because you are willing," "not greedy for money, but eager to serve; not lording it over those entrusted to you, but being examples. And when the Chief Shepherd appears, you will receive the crown of glory that will never fade away.

(1 Peter 5:2–4)

We desperately need to return to these principles and select leaders who will guide the church in the direction that is consistent with God's Word.

Exercise of Spiritual Gifts by the Membership

We [all] have different gifts, according to the grace given us.

Romans 12:6

God has given every person who has received His Spirit special spiritual gifts and abilities. His desire for us is that we will *"be fruitful and multiply"* (Genesis 9:21).

The man-made change in church structure in many churches has resulted in a loss of the purity of our faith and downplayed the enabling gifts of the Spirit in the believer's life. In turn, this has led to spiritual callousness, division, and barrenness, instead of holiness and fruitfulness.

When John the Baptist started his ministry he began with this astonishing warning:

The ax is already at the root of the trees, and every tree that does not produce good fruit will be cut down and thrown in the fire.

(Matthew 3:10)

He then continued telling them about the divine enabling planned for them:

I baptize you with water for repentance. But after me will come one who is more powerful than I ... He will baptize you with the Holy Spirit and with fire.

(Matthew 3:11)

This verse should prompt us to action! When working with new Christians, it is always a joy to see the enthusiasm and fire in them. Unfortunately, this fire is all too often quenched as they begin to mix with lukewarm believers.

AN EXCITING EXAMPLE

Confession and witnessing is a natural outgrowth of salvation; unless we as believers become involved for God, we will not see the reproductive action God brings about by his Spirit. And who can predict the far-reaching results when our spiritual giftedness is used? For example, in 1885 a man named Edward Kimble felt compelled to share his faith with a man who had sold him his shoes. He went back to the store and talked to the young man, who was open to receiving God's love. That clerk, Dwight L. Moody, later became a great evangelist.

A Frederick B. Meyer was so touched by D.L. Moody's bold preaching method and visible fire that he began a similar evangelistic ministry. While he was preaching, a young student by the name of Wilbur Chapman accepted Christ. Mr. Chapman later helped a young baseball player by the name of Billy Sunday to trust Christ. Sunday also became a great evangelist.

In 1924, Billy Sunday was invited to hold an evangelistic meeting in Charlotte, North Carolina, at which many people came to Christ. This crusade was repeated again some years later by an evangelist named Mordecai Hamm. It was there a young man named Billy Graham committed his life to Christ. And the rest is history.

In John 15, Jesus says He is the source of our strength and being in Him, we are meant to continually bring forth fruit. Jesus does not talk about natural fruitfulness but spiritual fruitfulness. He means that every Christian should be reproducing other Christians. While we cannot make anyone a Christian (only the Spirit can regenerate people), we can help them desire to become believers by our testimony. Jesus' desire is for us to live holy lives that will enable us to be fruitful for Him through the use of the spiritual gifts the Holy Spirit gives us.

A MINISTRY FOR ALL BELIEVERS

Now about spiritual gifts ... I do not want you to be ignorant ... There are different kinds of gifts but the same Spirit ... Now to each one the manifestation of the Spirit is given for the common good. To one ... wisdom, to another ... knowledge, to another faith, ... healing, ... miraculous powers.

You can read this in Romans 12, 1 Corinthians 12, and Ephesians 4. Today, we do not see these gifts much in evidence because the church in many places is no longer a body of ministers, but a group of consumers with few active in any way.

Jesus tells us we should edify and build each other up with psalms, hymns, and spiritual songs. We should admonish, instruct, encourage, and pray for each other. More typically in our churches, however, one person does all the talking and there is no opportunity to use our spiritual gifts for interaction, participation, or ministering to each other.

BELIEVERS MUST HAVE LIBERTY TO EXERCISE THEIR GIFTS

In a truly Christian church, we live by God's rules. Each believer is expected to be a minister. The Bible says that:

> *You also, like living stones, are being built into a spiritual house to be a holy priesthood, offering spiritual sacrifices acceptable to God through Jesus Christ.*
>
> (1 Peter 2:5)

A Christian church is designed to continue Christ's ministry; it acts as a body, with all of the believers ministering one to another as well as to the world.

Sadly, the responsibility of every believer to have and use his or her spiritual gifts is generally being neglected or discouraged in the churches of today.

SERIOUS LACK # 5

Genuine Love and Fellowship
Within the Body

This is His commandment, that we believe in the name
of His Son Jesus Christ, and love one another.

1 John 3:23 NASB

A TRANSFORMED PEOPLE

Have you ever gone to a church where you see no enthusiasm, no openness about faith or evidence of transformed personalities among the members? These churches are not based upon the salvation of the soul, but upon tradition and dead theology that may reach the mind without transforming the heart.

When we come to personal faith in Christ, God gives us a new heart, a new love, and a new joy. In the passage above, the New Testament Christians loved to meet with each other. They cared for each other and had praise upon their lips because of what God had done for them.

LOVE BASED UPON RELATIONSHIP

They even met during the week and were helping, caring and encouraging each other in both physical and spiritual needs. They met from house to house. This meant not only structured services but also a small group movement. No doubt, elders were the pastors of those small groups because in the description of elders we read they must be able to lead, able to teach, and given to hospitality.

The Bible gives us a large list of "relational commandments" such as loving, caring, praying, encouraging, and standing in for each other. The Christian life was never meant to be a life of individualism but of a caring community. As the world saw how much these Christians loved each other, some even selling their surplus possessions in order to help those who had needs, nonbelievers were drawn to the Christian faith.

MOTIVATED BY LOVE

"By this all men will know that you are my disciples, if you love one another" (John 13:35). To what extent must we love each other? *"As I have loved you, so you must love one another"* (John 13:34b).

This was Jesus' command and it speaks of love even to death for the body of Christ, which refers to all believers (1 John 3:16). Regarding the New Testament Church, we read:

> *All the believers were one in heart and mind. No one claimed that any of his possessions was his own, but they shared everything they had.*
>
> (Acts 4:32)

Where there is love there is God, and where there is unity there is power. Jesus emphasized, "Where two or three of you agree in prayer," meaning agreeing with God's will—not ours—we could move mountains. Could it be that, having lost Christ's presence, we also have lost direction for the church because we are no longer able to discern the mind and instructions of God? Have we failed to allow the Holy Spirit to control us and all of our actions?

CONTROLLED BY THE SPIRIT

The question we are raising is "What control does the Spirit have in the church today?" Is there room for flexibility in programs or for reform, or are doctrinal views set in stone? Some claim to have "forms of unity," but these are more like "forms of exclusivity" and continual darkness. How strong is the emphasis upon the spiritual rebirth, love for other believers, or a Christ-committed walk of its membership?

In Scripture we read:

> *Repent and be baptized, every one of you, in the name of Jesus Christ for the forgiveness of your sins. And you will receive the gift of the Holy Spirit.*
>
> (Acts 2:38)

God has given His gift of the Holy Spirit to those who obey Him (Acts 5:32).

What is the obedience Christ asks from us? Jesus requires that we come to Him, turn away from our old ways and trust Him to equip and enable us to live a life that is spiritually productive and pleasing to Him.

LOVE IN WELCOMING NEWCOMERS

In the early church, one of the requirements for being an elder was to practice hospitality to strangers (Romans 12:13; I Timothy 3:2). When a newcomer was recognized as a believer or had a letter of introduction, he or she would be warmly welcomed into the church.

That some churches today are no longer functioning by God's design and have lost sight of biblical methods of receiving new people is revealed by the awkwardness, or sometimes even blind awareness, with which they receive new people or visitors. If we require anything more of newcomers than that they belong to Christ it means Christ is no longer the all-sufficient One. The word "church" is taken from the Greek word *Koinonia,* which means fellowship; a sharing of Christ with each other.

Over the years, when my wife and I moved to a new town we would look for a church where we would feel welcome. In most churches we walked in as strangers and walked out the same, deeply disappointed. In some we were asked to leave our name and address; then we simply received a form letter in the mail.

In Romans 15:7, the apostle Paul writes: *"Welcome one another as Christ has welcomed you"* (ESV). The basis on which one should be welcomed into Christ's church is our oneness in Christ. Then why, in many local churches today, do so many regulations, restrictions, and reservations have to be met for one to be accepted as fellow believers in Christ? The reason is simple: many churches are no longer Christ-centered. They are rather centered on a particular doctrine or interpretation of Scripture. They seemingly have no interest in or tolerance for other views. Perhaps even the apostle Paul would have trouble being accepted in those churches today.

One of the criteria we were looking for as we visited those churches was the practical exposition of the Scripture, not the ideas, stories, or theological ideas of men. We also sought a church where the singing of the great psalms and hymns God has given to the church through the years had not been discarded; where prayer still had a central place; where the ministry of house groups was vital, and where there was a welcome to all followers of Christ.

In most churches, very few people spoke to us and we found

little welcome as believers. We had no friends in the community and it seemed many social clubs were more eager to receive one than the churches we visited.

God gave the Israelites very clear instructions as to how to receive strangers, and Jesus asked the church not to do anything less: *"Anyone who receives a righteous man ... [or] gives even a cup of cold water ... because he is my disciple ... he will certainly not lose his reward"* (Matthew 10:41–42), and *"I was a stranger and you invited me in"* (Matthew 25:35).

At one time we were involved in a church ministry that had people standing in the church foyer looking for strangers to welcome and invite them into their homes. New house groups were continually developing in that environment.

Another approach with which we were strongly impressed was one in which every new person was invited to visit in a coffee room with the pastor at the end of the service. While there, everyone was given a gift. The gift was a video presentation telling what the church believed and what it was all about. The church then had a visiting team to visit the newcomers within a week, welcoming and questioning them regarding their faith and to present fundamental Biblical truths. Many first-time visitors in that church came to Christ through that outreach. How could seekers ever say "no" to such a welcome, both into the church and into a small house group to which they were promptly invited?

Upon moving to another city, we finally found a church that met most of the criteria we had established. After months of attending, we were invited to someone's home. If I had not phoned the office, I wonder if the pastor would have ever contacted us. Even then, we were not fully received into that fellowship. We still were not treated fully as part of the church as we had not initiated the membership process and made it clear we gave full allegiance to their particular doctrinal views.

By contrast, the Bible gives only five conditions for membership in the church:

CHURCH ON THE ROCK

1. The first requirement is *repentance,* as given by Peter on the day of Pentecost when Jesus began his church: *"[Then] Peter said to them, 'repent'"* (Acts 2:38 NASB).
2. Then, there must be *an indication of a living faith* by confessing Jesus as their only means of salvation, as spoken by Peter: *"You are the Christ, the Son of the living God"* (Matthew 16:16).
3. Having expressed faith in Christ, they were to be evaluated by looking at their *Christian walk. "Just as you received Christ Jesus as Lord, continue to live in him"* (Colossians 2:6).
4. After having come to faith like Paul on the road to Damascus or the Ethiopian eunuch as other New Testament believers, we read they were baptized: *"Baptizing them in the name of the Father and of the Son and of the Holy Spirit"* (Matthew 28:19).
5. Since salvation means *obedience,* believers must continue to remain actively involved toward *spiritual growth,* as we read: *"Devoting themselves to the apostle's teaching and to fellowship, to the breaking of bread and to prayer"* (Acts 2:42 NASB).

The church Jesus intended us to have was meant to be an action group based on the basic requirements of the Christian faith. In some churches today we still hear messages about personal salvation. We hear few about a repentant lifestyle, growing into holiness, and continuing in the apostle's doctrines—all of which were meant to help each of us become doers of the Word and not church attendees only.

MEMBERSHIP CRITERIA

Who has given a church the right to make secondary, man-made requirements for membership such as forms of baptism, the timing of the rapture, eternal security, or how much one should contribute—requirements other than those the Lord has given us to become members of His Church? (Hebrews 6:2).

One often feels like a total outsider trying to break through a barrier in order to be accepted. This is being done by many churches at a time when they are willing to discard their hymnbooks in order to become more "seeker friendly."

It is clearly time to review our system of receiving new believers into fellowship and become more focused on God's requirements as stated in the Bible. After all, it is one's Christian walk that needs to be examined, not merely one's intellectual acknowledgement of a particular creed or collection of church rules. Otherwise, we may very well ask, "Whose church is it anyway?"

Evangelism and Missions

Therefore go and make disciples of all nations.
Matthew 28:19

Missions have become a sideline of many churches today as building programs have taken the priority. Many churches have become social centers, and many pastors are no longer shepherds. Biblical accuracy has taken a back seat to membership growth, and expository preaching has been replaced by opinions and stories of men.

It is only by Christ's Spirit and the new birth that new members can be added to the Church. A church therefore must qualify its new members as to having been baptized into Christ and being fully committed to Him by their witness for Christ and their lifestyle.

Jesus said:

> *But you will receive power when the Holy Spirit comes on you; and you will be my witnesses in Jerusalem, and in all Judea and Samaria, and to the ends of the earth.*
>
> (Acts 1:8)

LEADERSHIP SHOULD DEVELOP

> *The things you have heard me say in the presence of many witnesses entrust to reliable men who will also be qualified to teach others.*
>
> (2 Timothy 2:2)

Leadership within the church must continually develop and motivate new believers into living a witnessing lifestyle in order to maintain a growing and living church. A reproducing church is a healthy church. A healthy church does not need to conform to worldly marketing methods for growth because God has through His Spirit installed a divine method for reproduction—"*people winning people.*" When people become fully committed to the Lord, and have reached spiritual enthusiasm and maturity through proper nourishment, and are blessed by their fellowship they will become reproducing agents.

REPRODUCTION

> *As the Father has sent me, I am sending you.*
>
> (John 20:21)

Jesus chose and trained twelve disciples in a three year period. If leaders would train another twelve people over a similar period of time, imagine the duplication effect and the active ministry that would take place! A reproducing church will be a growing church!

What do believers need to have in order to be effective for ministry?

- Assurance of salvation and knowledge of the Word
- A personal walk with Christ
- Being filled with Christ's Spirit
- Having a real sense of belonging to a body
- Needing each other's gifts for teamwork in outreach
- Being able and willing to submit to authority
- Awareness of our high calling in Christ
- A love for each person as being most valuable to God
- A vision of the horrible outcome of sin and the reality of hell
- Learning to live a godly lifestyle
- Looking for the reward that is waiting for us in eternity

FRUIT BEARING

This is to my Father's glory, that you bear much fruit.
(John 15:8)

How can one attain these attributes? By coming together as believers, teaching and ministering to one another. The fact that many churches are not doing this is causing indescribable harm to the body of Christ. The body of Christ has become a group of lazy spectators instead of fruit-bearers. Instead of being learning centers, the churches have become entertainment or lecturing centers. Instead of sheep feeding stations, they have become kindergarten centers where believers can learn a new song and listen to a story. They are no longer schools for developing prophets, pastors, or evangelists, but are inactive gathering centers that no longer function under God's control. This is what is hindering true biblical church growth. This is what we must repent of.

Churches promote generous giving, but many times much of the funding is used for operating costs, leaving little for world missions or ministry to the needy.

Often, over ninety percent of a church's budget is spent on itself. The overspending on exorbitant salaries and great buildings has discouraged many people in their giving. Some are even reluctant to join a church. Most churches do not seek volunteers but rather hire employees.

The low priority given to missions and evangelism in many churches is yet another characteristic of a church that is lacking.

Sensitivity to Concerns of the Elderly

[The righteous] will still bear fruit in old age.
Psalm 92:14

If a church conforms to the ways, music and methods of this world in order to attract the outsider, such an approach invariably leads to ignoring the opinions and feelings of the elderly members of the congregation.

Other churches may lay a stronger emphasis upon the quality of the proclamation of the message, the standards of accepting new members or the content of the songs being sung. Perhaps in this we cannot please the same people in the same service, so why not meet at different times? But why are so many elderly people suddenly forced to accept a new form of service when it was they who built the church and maintained it through the years? Why do they have to come to church at an early and inconvenient time in order not to be disturbed by a new style of worship?

If we love each other, there needs to be consideration so that needs of different age groups, *including* the elderly, are being met, and people are not being turned off by what others want the church to be.

> *The young will rise up against the old, the base against the honorable ... Youths oppress my people, women rule over them. O my people, your guides lead you astray; they turn you from the path.*
>
> (Isaiah 3:5b, 12)

Nor should we expect the Lord to bless us when we ignore or walk over the elderly in order to keep the young people and to bring the unbelievers into the church. Our motive does not justify our deeds. It is the Lord's blessing we must be striving for, not men's ideas and conformity to the world in order to enlarge the church.

Many older believers, apart from the one-hour service, live in spiritual loneliness, frustration, and rejection. They are given no opportunity for participation. Even if they were, they would no longer know what to do. As many new songs are being used, they sit or stand in a pew with sad faces, with the expression of someone who is sick. The old familiar, doctrinally-rich hymns and gospel songs they love are no longer sung or heard—in order that the church can be "contemporary."

IT CREATES RESTLESSNESS

This situation has caused a great deal of restlessness among believers, particularly the elderly. Many have given up on the traditional church and are now following TV or radio pastors. Some of these pastors have a good sound message and are strengthening believers throughout the world.

Others have turned to the house church movement, hoping this might be the answer. Still others are, out of desperation, being taken in by the mega-churches that are appearing all over the country, where tradition has long been done away with. Many of these are like fast-food restaurants, with lots of appeal but little real nutrition.

Then there are those who have completely stopped going to church because of deep hurts and disillusionment. They have concluded that a lacking church is as bad as no church. My heart goes out to these people, as I've gone through all these stages. But I still believe there is hope for the church, because, in spite of it all, I have discovered that God is real and He cares—for the church and also for the elderly.

Nevertheless, disregard for the concerns and feelings, insights and wisdom of the elderly in today's church has robbed her of much value.

PART ONE:

The State of the Church

Section B

Distressing Conditions *Very* Evident
in Today's Church

DISTRESSING CONDITION # 1

Culture-driven Approach to Ministry

*Do not conform any longer to the pattern of this world,
but be transformed.*

Romans 12:2

Many churches as well as Christians today have conformed to this world. Deeds that are called "sin" in the Bible are now condoned or called "human abnormalities," and we pretend God will tolerate them. The main goal of many churches is increased membership; accordingly they use marketing methods to draw unbelievers into membership. They call holiness "unattainable," disobedience is "freedom from legalism or superstition," and sin is "relevant" or perhaps a "defect in one's personality."

The church that Jesus intended us to have was never meant to be an evangelism center primarily. Believers are to do evangelism, but the biblical concept of the ministry of all believers seems to have become obsolete. Thus, in order to maintain church growth, many churches have resorted to a therapeutic gospel and a cosmetic form of Christianity of which people and their needs are at the center instead of God and His glory.

Many have adopted the theory that "if it feels good, it must be good." We seem to care more about people's psychological needs than about their spiritual well-being. Many go to church for "self-fulfillment," and not for instruction in righteousness or in how to have a godly walk.

There also seems to have been a revolution within most churches over the choice of music. In order to imitate the mega church concept and wanting to become the most popular church in town, many churches have done away with the use of the biblical psalms or their existing hymnbooks. They feel the new style of singing will keep the youth and make the church more visitor-friendly.

The new gospel that is also being gradually introduced is one that asks for little commitment, displays little fear of God, but deals with much concern of self-fulfillment. Thus we do not want songs about the blood, Christian warfare, suffering, judgment, or hell. Jesus has to become an attractive option—a "buddy" who can give you much gain without pain, much comfort instead of taking up a cross. Instead of being the only way for a whole new life, He becomes an "added benefit."

In order to present an attractive gospel, some feel we need to bring in the band and do away with the old songs. We are now turning to new lyrics or love songs to Jesus with gestures and styles that will appeal to the emotions. It is hard to see how this fits with Psalm 19:14: *"May the words of my mouth and the meditation of my heart be pleasing in your sight, O LORD, my Rock and my Redeemer."*

In our churches we have spectators as well as followers, because church membership in many places is based upon people answering a few questions and agreeing to a man-made creed or statement of faith, instead of on the fact God has personally transformed them through the new birth. Yes, many have made human standards for church membership but do little searching for true evidences of salvation and separation from the world in the lives of their members.

A "COMFORTABLE" GOSPEL

In the church today, we bemoan a great falling away. It is not the falling away of people, primarily. Many times the leaders of the church have fallen away from God. We have adopted earthly methods of church growth and turned, just like in Ezekiel's days, to a smooth, non-offensive gospel in order to keep the flock. This gospel says, "Just believe in Jesus or in the church and you'll be saved." This message, however, ignores the whole counsel of God, which speaks of repenting from former sins, of taking up our cross, and of being conformed to the image of Christ by the refining work of the Holy Spirit. The message we hear today is basically silent about the reality of hell, the signs of the times, and the sins of the society in which we live. Many times corruption within the church is quickly swept under the carpet. Church discipline is rarely heard of in our churches.

With our man-made changes in the structure of many churches, we have lost the purity of the faith and downplayed the enabling gifts of the Spirit in the believer's life. Thus, we have caused and tolerated spiritual callousness, division and barrenness instead of holiness and fruitfulness.

When we hear of a church doing something that has brought in thousands, we run to pick up some new human ideas. Instead of simply turning to God in order to get our instructions from His Word, we seek human wisdom.

IS JESUS IN CONTROL?

Not only have the hymnbooks disappeared from many of today's churches, but so have the Bibles, the evening services, and the weekly prayer meetings. Perhaps these meetings no longer exist because we have made them so boring that they weren't worth attending. Also, as discussed earlier, by becoming a "one man show," churches ignore God's commandments. *"You have a fine way of setting aside the commands of God in order to observe your own traditions"* (Mark 7:9).

Many congregations that are not functioning by Christ's design have distressed and overloaded their pastors to the extent that they are suffering spiritual depression and physical burnout.

Informality has been instrumental in killing the vitality of the church. Now, by changing the Sunday morning services to being "seeker friendly" and watering down the message, we are destroying it even further. When designing the building of His church God clearly rejected the use of the wisdom and methods of this world. The Bible warns us: *"For my thoughts are not your thoughts, neither are your ways my ways,' declares the LORD"* (Isaiah 55:8). *"I will destroy the wisdom of the wise; the intelligence of the intelligent I will frustrate"* (1 Corinthians 1:19).

It is time for the church to return to biblical principles in obedience to the Lord both in structure and operation. It is time to again become a church energized by Christ's supernatural power rather than by human efforts.

COUNTERFEIT GOSPELS

Many churches are becoming merely lecture, social, or entertainment centers. We would do well to heed Paul's warning to the Galatians when he expresses his astonishment that they had already turned to another gospel, which is really no gospel at all

(Galatians 1:6–10). Today, in order to appeal to our self-centered culture, we see many twisted "gospels" such as:

- Salvation without separation
- Justification without sanctification
- Faith without obedience
- Belief without discipleship
- Perception of spiritual gain without pain or suffering
- Having Christ without following His teachings
- Seeking revival without repentance
- Gatherings without spiritual food or inspiration

The drive to appeal to our culture has produced harmful and dangerous trends including the "seeker-sensitive" and "purpose-driven" approaches, as well as the invasion of the church by the pervasive and growing emergent church, even in evangelical churches.

As Protestant churches become more commercially oriented rather than spiritually sensitive, they are gradually being drawn into a worldwide church. They are willing to consider the one-church concept under the slogan of "Christian unity." In order to gain even greater status, recognition, and power, Christian standards of discipleship and the old hymns that deeply describe biblical salvation, suffering and the Spirit-filled life are being removed. This future church has cultural appeal as well as gifted "miracle working" pulpiteers who are more inclined to preach a pseudo-gospel than declare the whole counsel of God to the church. Greatness, power, and compromise in order to gain a false unity with a very shallow concept of salvation and strong pulpit control are but the early signs of the establishment of the end-time unified church.

A "CALLED OUT" ASSEMBLY

The word *church* comes from the Greek *ecclesia,* which means "an assembly of called-out ones." It is never used in the New

Testament to mean a denomination or building. When the church stoops to making its gatherings attractive to the non-Christian culture, major problems are the result. The biblical church gathering is one in which *believers* worship God, fellowship with one another, study the Word, and are equipped for service. It is not the place for evangelism, primarily, but rather exists to equip believers to do the work of evangelism out in the world. Therefore, the great concern should not be to make church gatherings feel comfortable to the unconverted through worldly music, entertainment, and casual sloppy dress.

A culture-driven approach to ministry immeasurably harms the church.

Clergy/Laity Structure

Not lording it over those entrusted to you, but being examples to the flock.

1 Peter 5:3

Because of carnal human control instead of Spirit-directed leadership in ministry, we have greatly diluted God's intent and degraded the church. We have divided the body into clergy and laity, causing churches to be divided and turning masses away from this man-made institution we call "church." All this is because we have neglected Christ's design and instructions for the building of His church.

HOW IT ALL CAME TO PASS

In the early church, true followers of Christ did not fit in with the world until the Roman Emperor Constantine became a "Christian." In approximately 330 AD, he took up the cause for Christians and instituted a state-organized church with all its trappings, including liturgy and hierarchy. Soon, all the prominent government leaders and the masses declared themselves Christian. They brought with them into the church many heathen concepts such as temple worship, worship of the mother and child image, compulsory offerings, and the high prominence of the religious priesthood. Eventually, the state-sponsored church gave control to men who claimed to have authority from Jesus Christ but who kept the Bible away from ordinary people, thus making the leadership free to "interpret" the Bible as they pleased.

FAITHFUL BELIEVERS

Then, small groups of Christians who faithfully held on to the New Testament faith and refused to participate in those heathen influences and the syncretism of the state-church's practices became the persecuted "cults." The established church went into the dark ages for 1200 years. Severe taxation, the sale of "pardons" for forgiveness of sins, releases to get loved ones out of purgatory, and praying to the saints were just a few of the many corruptions of the newly commercialized state-endorsed church of those days.

REFORMATION

From 1200 AD to 1600 AD, men such as Wycliffe, Huss, Tyndale, Luther, Calvin, Zwingli, and others saw the abuse of leadership, with its withholding and misinterpretation of Scripture, and led the way to reformation against the established church. They sought a return to biblical truth by translating and printing the Bible in the language of the common people. Luther principally fought for two things, namely: justification by faith—not by the purchase of indulgences or the absolution of a priest—and the priesthood of all believers with no division of clergy and laity. Mission-consciousness began to grow and many signs of new life appeared within the new Protestant church.

Not free from carnality, however, these new churches still had difficulty giving up the hierarchical concepts, and maintained that people could become "Christianized" simply by church loyalty—the only thing expected of them. Although the Word of God had now come to the people, the ministry was still kept to a few clergy. These men, mostly former priests, were not willing to give up their positions of prominence and prestige.

Continued Persecutions

Fortunately, however, from the earliest times of the Roman church and even after the Reformation, there were always remnant groups who disagreed with the religion of the "established" church. For them, Christianity was not merely a creed but a Holy, Spirit-directed way of life. Salvation for them did not come through the church or the sacraments but only through Jesus Christ. Not surprisingly, these people were hunted down by the dominant Protestants and Catholics alike and were either killed as heretics or forced to move to another country.

The Protestant churches took over many Catholic Church buildings as well. All this became a political shift and an organized attempt to remove papal power. These Protestants established their own authority instead of embracing the freedom of ministry that Jesus had promised to all believers. Then later, when religious freedom became widely accepted, catechisms, prayer books, and creeds were developed and placed into use, thus hindering the people from obtaining other biblical insights and sources beyond the central control of the church hierarchy.

MAINTAINERS OF THE FAITH

Yet, by His grace, God has kept remnant groups alive through the centuries who have maintained the true meaning of salvation by faith, the rule of Christ, and the priesthood of all believers. Their quest was the freedom of living out their faith in holiness and obedience to truth, even in the face of death.

Protestants as well as Catholics, in blind loyalty to their own churches, burned many of these dear people at the stake. It was these remnant groups and individuals who truly upheld the Christian faith. They were not blinded by the established church of their times, whose followers all too often, in their religious blindness, used the sword to further their cause.

In these remnant groups, every believer was meant to minister and knew what it meant to suffer for their faith. There was no distinction between pastor and layman. Personal salvation and total obedience to Christ's teachings formed their lifestyle, and this included "nonresistance" and believer's baptism. Their devotion was to the call of God, not to the dictates of a political or religious power group. These remnant groups were at that time the true salt of the earth as they kept alive the truth of our Christian faith.

They come to us through history under names such as the Huguenots, Anabaptists, Friends, Brethren, Moravians, Waldesians, Bohemians, and many more. These were called in their day "disturbers of the peace," heretics, agitators, fanatics, and covenant breakers. Despite hardship and persecution, they kept a light burning for the historic Christian faith.

They maintained that salvation comes by personal faith in Christ, not by the sacraments, and that faith comes by hearing the Word preached, not by adherence to a human creed or by loyalty to a man-controlled organization. They rightly believed that our complete sufficiency is in Christ, not in additional ceremonial deeds or additional experiences. Their emphasis was upon a holy walk and separation from the ways and methods of the world, even within the structure of the church. These "heretics" were folk of whom the world was not worthy. They were the upholders of the true Christian faith. Although churches now give lip service to these truths, many still run the church as a business with hirelings and great financial requirements.

GOD'S REMNANT PEOPLE

In every church, we may still find a remnant of true believers, those who obey God and are committed to Him. They see no distinction between pastors or laity, a specific organization or creed. For them, there are only two kinds of people, those who have God's witness within them and those who need it.

Christianity for them is not individualism or seeking after materialism, but being willing to share what they have with those in need, caring, praying, and loving each other as Christ has loved them. This is living out their faith in holiness and fear before a holy God, and if need be, before the ridicule of others, even in the church. For them, Christianity is bearing a cross, not following the crowd.

A MIXED CHURCH

Because King Solomon married many foreign wives in disobedience to the Lord, Israel's worship of God became mixed with other religions. This put Israel on a wrong course spiritually.

In the New Testament Church, history repeated that phenomenon when the Roman Emperor Constantine endorsed the Christian religion. The persecuted church suddenly became a state-sponsored church, and many heathen concepts were at that time introduced into Christian worship.

- The church became man-controlled
- Infant baptism became compulsory
- Worship of Mary and other saints became accepted
- A professional priesthood was established
- Unbiblical ways and means of raising money were practiced
- Salvation was declared to be possible only through the church

Then came the Reformation, for which the main issues were:

- Rejection of raising money by the sale of indulgences
- Salvation by faith, not by works or purchase of financial pardons
- Access to the Bible for all believers, not just the leaders

But many Protestant churches never became fully restored:

- They continued to be a man-controlled system
- They ignored Christ's standard of holiness and discipleship
- They continued religious manipulation

IT IS HIS CHURCH

Biblically speaking, it was Jesus who talked about "His Church" but many of today's churches are ultimately governed by one man at a remote denominational headquarters, with the result that local churches are tightly controlled both doctrinally and structurally. This often limits the church or even the pastor from changing anything, even changes that are clearly biblical or Spirit-led.

God wants His Spirit to control the church. A church that is "man-controlled" cannot be "God-controlled" because God will not share His glory with any individual, pope, priest, or organization. A spirit-controlled church is a miraculously-formed church; it is a divine organism that reveals the power, love, and the presence of God.

Today, churches have made employment out of ministry, hiring pastors out of schools that teach pre-conceived biblical concepts and human skills. These schools give pastors very little freedom to search the Scriptures under guidance of the Spirit and to offer their hearers the things they have learned from the Lord. For many pastors who are under theological restraints and restrictions, ministry can lead to great frustration; they are constrained from saying what the Spirit wants them to say.

The apostle Paul in 1 Corinthians 11:22 warned new believers not to despise or take lightly what God intended the church to be, as was indicated earlier.

HUMAN LEADERSHIP VERSUS GOD'S CONTROL

Like Israel of old, many in the church today want to follow an attractive and motivating leader; he is not a king—but he takes charge—we call him the "senior pastor."

Not atypically he gradually gets control of a humanly-designed eldership board and then begins to basically rule the church as he wishes. When this happens, the church stands or falls by one man—their pastor. The problem is that when man is in control, the Holy Spirit cannot be in control because God will not be controlled by men. Many times, if such a single leader falters, the entire church goes down.

Singular leadership, pulpit control, and making God's people spectators instead of ministry partakers—all hinder spiritual growth and diminish responsiveness and sensitivity to God's leadership within his people and throughout the church.

Human control generally removes the mystery and prevents the church's functioning as an organism. It reduces its spirituality and causes men to accept earthly and deceiving methods, just to keep the system in existence.

EVANGELISM AS GOD INTENDED

Paul challenged Timothy to "do the work of an evangelist" (2 Timothy 4:5). Jesus directed and used evangelism when He send out his disciples and when He preached the gospel of the Kingdom and healed the sick as they went from village to village (Luke 9:1–6).

Those believers who are gifted as evangelists could function as such if the church were open to this and if the church were an inviting place that warmly received new Christians and offered teachings for their growth. However, in most churches where the work is primarily done by paid clergy, enthusiasm for and direct involvement in ministry has dissipated. Many churches seek growth by making the services more appealing but have no vision for activating *all* believers into ministry. As a result, the gift of evangelism becomes buried or is left up to the independent practice of an occasional believer. It is only by going back to the basic biblical, structured design of the church in outreach and first love this can change.

Many books have been published on church growth, but little or no emphasis has been given to stirring up the gift of evangelism, which ought to be the passion of every believer who is meant to be a minister of reconciliation.

MORE REFORMATION NEEDED

From the time that Emperor Constantine institutionalized the church, many things were put in place that even the Reformation did not remove. This incomplete Reformation is still causing decay in the church. We must ask God to help us so that we may further *reform* from:

Re-instituting the Old Testament priesthood (1 Peter 2:4).
Eliminating the ministry of all believers (1 Peter 5:2).

Forming congregations into spectator audiences (1 Peter 2:9).

Organizing the body of Christ into a clergy and laity format (1 Peter 2:4).

Reducing spiritual growth in most believers (Ephesians 4:12–14).

Minimizing the use of spiritual ministry gifts (Ephesians 4:11).

SLAVES OR FRANCHISEES?

With the introduction of organized religion, the church in many places is no longer under Christ's direction but men's control. Every denomination seems to be based upon a creed or constitution that describes what it believes and encourages the Bible to be read from that perspective. There seems to be no room for other insights or for altering the church's structure.

Many denominations have their own schools of theology to train young preachers to serve their network of churches. The clergy as well as the members are taught to read and interpret the Bible from the denomination's perspective.

These young preachers usually are first assigned to a small church where they work under a senior pastor. Upon proven ability and allegiance to their "system," they may move to a larger church. These men generally have little latitude to consider other insights into Scripture unless they change affiliation, which often means losing pension and other benefits. Can we say of such that there is freedom in serving Christ?

These and many other unbiblical conditions are a reflection of the clergy/laity denominational mindset.

Focus on Numerical Growth

*Man looks on the outward appearance, but the Lord
looks on the heart.*

1 Samuel 16:7

When membership is based on mere "Church-ianity" in order to increase attendance and encourage membership growth, many churches lower Christ's requirements for salvation and a truly Christian lifestyle. Such churches seldom speak of our Savior's call for new birth, holiness, discipleship, or walking in newness of life.

This leads to people assuming they have salvation because they are so deeply involved in church activities. It is their church they are excited about rather than the Lord. Their spiritual blindness gives them a church addiction. They wouldn't care whether their church preaches salvation or ever sees any conversions because they have been blinded toward these essentials. For them, church growth is all about numbers, and they consider the best church members to be those who most actively support the system.

When churches grow large, they are tempted to enter into a numbers game, losing personal touch with their attendees and sometimes simply treating them as merchandise (2 Peter 2:13). The pastor can no longer be a shepherd as the Bible directs him to be. Many times, he becomes the church's business manager and CEO, often being paid in accordance with his ability in those areas.

Some churches or denominations even become like clubs with more social benefits to maintain their audience. Their object is seemingly not to win, mature, and disciple believers, but simply to cater to their members, using other powers and methods to draw a crowd.

MAKING ONE TWICE A CHILD OF HELL

Woe to you teachers of the law ... You travel over land and sea to win a single convert, and when he becomes one, you make him twice as much a son of hell as you are.
(Matthew 23:15)

As we know, unless people are personally born again, they are on their way to hell. Jesus told the religious leaders of His day that they gave people a false concept of salvation, namely loyalty to their system. Today, in our eagerness to increase church membership and attendance, we also often fail to look for a transformed life as evidence of salvation. Many people confuse church membership with being a Christian. Churches, having accepted the unconverted as members, now also have to tolerate lukewarm or carnal believers. The apostle Paul declared, *"Woe unto me if I do not preach the gospel"* (1 Corinthians 9:16) and Jesus also emphatically requested, *"Make Me disciples,"* so what do we preach? We preach an assumed "soft and easy"

Christianity in order to attract people instead of a challenge to become Christ's disciples?

For many people, being a Christian simply means belonging to a church—attending regularly and offering financial support. Most churches, in return, consider such people to be members in good standing. Many churchgoers have been deceived and have never been taught the true meaning of being a Christian.

Here are some facts that are typically overlooked in churches that strive for numerical growth at any cost.

RELATIONSHIP BEFORE KNOWLEDGE

Being born of the Spirit is how Jesus describes becoming a Christian: *"That which is born of the flesh is flesh, and that which is born of the Spirit is spirit"* (John 3:6, KJV).

Many churches talk about Christ but do not have Christ's message. Jesus clearly taught that we could never enter into a relationship with Him unless we first become spiritually reborn (John 3:3). Being spiritually born into the family of God must never be taken for granted. We must know beyond a shadow of a doubt that we experienced it. The Bible clearly challenges us towards personal self examination on this matter. Many churches encourage knowledge of and hope that spiritual life will eventually follow.

SPIRITUAL GROWTH—NOT INFORMATION

Be ye doers of the word, and not hearers only.

(James 1:22 KJV)

After birth comes growth, but we can never grow unless we first have become alive in Christ. Many will seek to live by the Golden Rule, but it is Christ within us that is imperative. Having received Christ's Spirit will enable us to live according to His teaching and in newness of life.

GOD FIRST

Seek ye first the kingdom of God, and his righteousness.
(Matthew 6:33, KJV)

Church activities should not be mistaken for kingdom activities. Many Christians and churches do very little to bring others into the Christian faith and therefore do not extend the kingdom of God. Those who only have social concerns give evidence that they have lost sight of the realities of God's kingdom. God's kingdom only grows when people become passionately filled with Christ's love for others.

DISCIPLESHIP—NOT JUST BELIEVING

Therefore go and make disciples of all nations, baptizing ... and teaching them to obey everything I have commanded you.
(Matthew 28:19–20)

Seeing others come to Christ is a basic mandate of being fruitful for every Christian. Some churches never see any new converts in their midst because they do not preach conversion. A disciple is a person who has accepted the Lord, is maturing in the faith, and lives in obedience to Christ's teachings.

ACTIONS—NOT ONLY WORDS

If anyone would come after me, he must deny himself and take up his cross and follow me.
(Matthew 16:24)

"Easy or simple believism" has removed an essential part of being Christ-followers. Many young people have left the

Christian faith because they have never been taught the real meaning of what enthusiastic living for Jesus is all about. For them, the joy of following Christ was never properly presented, therefore faith has little meaning or challenge. They may conclude faith is for the elderly and not relevant to them.

Others Before Self

Everyone looks out for his own interests, not those of Jesus Christ.

(Philippians 2:21)

In the "latter days," the Bible says, men will be "lovers of pleasure more than lovers of God." Love for each other will also fade, because many believers as well as churches will have motives that are materialistic and not related to obedience to God.

It is by being in community in small groups that we learn to care for each other. It was Christ's command we should love, care, and encourage each other constantly. A church giving only lip service to this mandate and emphasizing only congregational gatherings is like a car without gas—both are empty and useless.

Freewill—Not Compulsory

Each man should give what he has decided in his heart to give, not reluctantly or under compulsion, for God loves a cheerful giver.

(2 Corinthians 9:7)

Many churches promote only "storehouse tithing" as a means of raising money. But Moses said, "You are to receive the offering for me [God] from each man whose heart prompts him to give" (Exodus 25:2). The Bible clearly teaches us that: *"Denying ...*

worldly lusts, we should live soberly, righteously, and godly, in this present world" (Titus 2:12 KJV).

This means separating ourselves from a worldly lifestyle. If that were done, many could give a lot more than a tithe, but they use tithing as an excuse to do no more.

Teaching biblical truths and principles such as the above may not result in large attendance growth today, but it would produce obedient believers.

Unbiblical Criteria for Membership

Many, like us, have belonged to the church for years. As babies, we were baptized into the church. Growing older, we confirmed to the creeds of the church, but this did not make us a Christian. All these were special events, but when someone asks us when we had personally accepted Jesus we were stunned. This requirement was never presented to us but merely assumed.

I, on the contrary, have often wondered how a church can reject a non-member's vote when he is a true follower of Jesus. Does the Bible make a distinction between being committed attendees or church members when both belong to Christ? Can a church set additional requirements other than those Christ has set for belonging to Christ?

Some are unconcerned about their salvation, believing that it is God who does the choosing. They say there is nothing they can do about salvation, and if they are meant to be saved, they will be. Others will leap to the conclusion that eventually we all will get there, because God is a God of love.

Masses of both groups are in the church and are even considered members in good standing. They do not know that being a Christian means having a living relationship with God. Church membership has given many a false hope and a wrong understanding of salvation.

Thousands faithfully go to church but have little idea what it means to belong to Christ. They feel that their church will vouch for them when they leave this earth. They have never been informed that there is something that Christ requires of them in order to belong to Him, namely to be justified through the personal acceptance of Christ's atonement.

They are misinformed by having been led to believe that going to church is all that is required of them. In reality they are dead in their trespasses and sin. They feel that simply confessing their sin is enough, without ever experiencing the new life that Jesus has to offer.

Confusing church membership with salvation is disastrous especially when it is implied by many churches that there is no salvation outside their church. Even Jesus never asked his followers to join an organization but rather to follow Him and become His disciples.

Salvation:	Discipleship:
Is God's gift	Is our gratitude
Is an inward experience	Is an outward commitment
Is free	Is a commitment
Gives a white robe	Gives a uniform

Is receiving a shepherd	Is being under command
Comes by believing	Comes by obedience
Provides forgiveness of sins	Gives a reward in heaven

This is a matter with eternal repercussions. Sadly, multitudes of church people are completely unaware of what the Lord requires of them. For many, being a Christian merely means joining and going to church. This is not the intention for the body of Christ, nor will it provide salvation.

"How shall we escape if we ignore such a great salvation?" (Hebrews 2:3).

A HUMBLE LIFESTYLE

The Bible challenges us to live our lives in a humble manner that is distinct from the world. We are called to put God's interests before all our own objectives. Jesus gave us the Great Commandment as well as the Great Commission. The first priority is to love God and then those who have needs and live around us. Even a church treasury should first be used to help the needy and secondly to meet the needs of the church.

Then comes the Great Commission. Missions ought to be a central concern in the heart of every believer as well as the church. Today this attitude also is changing and the passion for reaching those who have never heard in many places around the world is being reduced to mere social action. James, the brother of Jesus, wrote: *"What good is it, my brothers, if a man claims to have faith but has no deeds? Can such faith save him?"* (James 2:14).

Rather than making requirements for membership today, we need to repent and conform to the requirements for the church that are clearly set forth in the Word of God.

We cannot attain such biblical standards in our human strength, but Jesus' abiding presence by His Spirit will enable us to keep His commandments even as He kept His Father's commandments by abiding in His love.

- He wants His followers to be His light in a world of darkness (Matthew 5:14).
- He wants His people to extend His kingdom on earth (Matthew 5:13).
- He wants every believer to have His Spirit's fullness and power (Acts 1:8).
- He wants all of us to reveal Him in all our actions (2 Corinthians 5:20).
- He wants believers to be a witness in each community (John 12:32).

A NOTE ABOUT THE SACRAMENTS IN RELATION TO MEMBERSHIP

Before Jesus returned to heaven, He gave his followers several symbolic observances that would replace Old Testament rituals. Two of these were communion and baptism.

In the Old Testament, the Passover was a meal of remembrance for what the Lord had done for Israel when He delivered them from their bondage in Egypt.

Jesus introduced His followers to the communion table so they would commemorate their deliverance from the bondage of sin through His sacrifice on the cross.

Israel was connected to God, their Jehovah, through a covenant relationship. Old Testament prophets, however, had already foretold that the day was coming that God would make a New Covenant that included Gentiles as well as Jews.

A Jew entered into the Old Covenant relationship with God by birth; the sign of this relationship was circumcision. We, as New Covenant believers, enter into this relationship with God by accepting Christ's offer of salvation, which brings spiritual birth. As a sign of this New Covenant relationship, the Bible teaches us to be baptized.

SACRAMENT ABUSE

Both the communion meal and water baptism are mere symbols of what Jesus has done for us. These sacraments or ordinances were meant to be used by the church universal; they are not to be confused with conditions of church membership. For example, the communion table is to be open to all believers, not for church members only, because it is not the table of any particular church, but the *Lord's* Table.

Neither are these sacraments to be confused as acts needed for salvation; the apostle Paul teaches us clearly when it comes to circumcision or baptism, Christ alone is the only source of our salvation, not sacraments, and that:

> *In him you were also circumcised, in the putting off of the sinful nature, not with circumcision done by the hands of men but with the circumcision done by Christ.*
> (Colossians 2:11)

And he even added ...

> *For Christ did not send me to baptize, but to preach the gospel.*
> (1 Corinthians 1:17)

> *Not laying again the foundation of repentance ... Instruction about baptisms, the laying on of hands, the resurrection of the dead.*
> (Hebrews 6:1–2)

It is our spiritual baptism *into* Christ that is important. It can only come when we submit ourselves fully and wholeheartedly to Christ.

> *Make every effort to keep the unity of the Spirit through the bond of peace. There is one body and one Spirit—just as you were called to one hope when you were called—one Lord, one faith, one baptism.*
>
> (Ephesians 4:3–6)

THE BAPTISM THAT IS IMPORTANT

It was John the Baptist who showed forth his understanding of what the coming of the Messiah was all about when he said: *"I baptize you with water for repentance. But after me will come one who is more powerful than I ... He will baptize you with the Holy Spirit and with fire"* (Matthew 3:11).

Have you ever met someone of whom it was said "they are truly on fire for the Lord?" What characterizes such a person? They have enthusiasm, eagerness to serve, willingness to sacrifice, a desire to witness for the Lord, and are not easily discouraged.

THE KEY

The key to living for Christ is not merely accepting Jesus for salvation but a wholehearted willingness to follow and serve Him. Listen to what the apostle Peter had to say to those who were gathered on the day of Pentecost:

> *John baptized with water, but in a few days you will be baptized with the Holy Spirit. Repent and be baptized, every one of you, in the name of Jesus Christ for the forgiveness of your sins [Cleansing]. And you will receive the gift of the Holy Spirit.*
>
> (Acts 1:5, 2:38)

Jesus Himself emphasized this condition of following and receiving the Spirit when He said: *"If you love me, you will obey what I command. And I will ask the Father, and he will give you another Counselor to be with you forever"* (John 14:15, 16).

The baptism we practice in many of our churches today is a formality of church membership. It is paired together with a shallow concept of salvation. Little consideration is given to the importance of producing fruit and living in the newness of life, which results from an inward transformation.

RESULTS OF COMMITMENT

"If anyone is thirsty, let him come to me and drink. Whoever believes in me, as the Scripture has said, streams of living water will flow from within him." By this he meant the Spirit, whom those who believed in him were later to receive.

(John 7:37–39)

These were the words Jesus spoke of those who would be empowered by His Spirit. The critics of the New Testament Church took notice of this when the Spirit first descended.

"When they saw the courage of Peter and John and realized that they were unschooled, ordinary men, they were astonished and they took note that these men had been with Jesus" (Acts 4:13).

In the Bible, we read that when the Holy Spirit filled the new believers, others were filled with awe. Believers had a tremendous love for each other and their testimony made such an impact that the church grew by the thousands—something we see happening in other countries today. The preaching was about salvation together with following Jesus. From Paul's ministry we read: *"Many of those who believed now came and openly confessed their evil deeds"* (Acts 19:18).

Yes it was not just the tongues of fire that indicated their baptism with the Holy Spirit and fire, but boldness, fearlessness, love, and great miracles manifested themselves. This church became known as "people who turned the world upside down" (Acts 17:6).

SIGNS OF THE NEW COVENANT

The receiving of Christ's Spirit is the sign and evidence that we have entered into a New Covenant relationship with God (Jeremiah 31; Ephesians 1:14). The coming of His Spirit upon all believers was promised in the Old Testament and is now fulfilled in our times.

While the Old Covenant was meant primarily for the Jew, the New Covenant is available to all believers, Jew, Greek, or even Barbarian. It is for male as well as female (Colossians 3:11; Galatians 3:28).

Jesus was very clear when He said to Nicodemus, *"That which is born of flesh is flesh; and that which is born of the Spirit is spirit."* To become a believer is not a natural occurrence but a supernatural event in which the Holy Spirit places a person into the family of God (John 1:12); this is the baptism that transforms.

> *We have not received the spirit of the world but the Spirit who is from God, that we may understand what God has freely given us ... The man without the Spirit does not accept the things that come from the Spirit of God, for they are foolishness to him.*
>
> (1 Corinthians 2:12, 14)

POWER TO CHANGE

The baptism Jesus offers to those who obey Him (Acts 5:32) will give the power to break the chains that bind us. Concepts like being "politically correct" or being "seeker friendly" do not further the gospel. Rather, the gospel is furthered by a holy boldness that comes through the Spirit's fullness. That will draw people to Christ. Believers who are delivered from a comfortable lifestyle as part of the world system display the evidences that will draw others to Christ.

The Bible speaks of the importance of the baptism *into* Jesus with the receiving of the Holy Spirit (Ephesians 4:6). This baptism is different from the baptism of John the Baptist or what many churches offer today. John's baptism was a baptism of repentance; the baptism of many churches is simply a rite of passage to membership. Being baptized *into* Jesus is first of all a baptism of personal faith in Jesus (Matthew 11:28). Secondly, it is a declaration that the old life died with Christ and of commitment to living in the newness of life (Matthew 7:21). It was from among these regenerate people who were full of the Spirit that elders and deacons were to be chosen (Acts 6:3).

So, in light of the above, baptism and participation at the Lord's Table are never be viewed simply as conditions for membership. To make them such is unbiblical.

As a summary of the shortcomings of the church of today, please carefully consider the following diagram.

PRESENT DAY CHURCH SHORTCOMINGS IN DIAGRAM FORM

THE CHURCH OF HUMAN DESIGN

For those who live by the flesh, do things according to the flesh ... The carnal mind cannot please God ... for it is enmity unto Him.

(Romans 8:5-8)

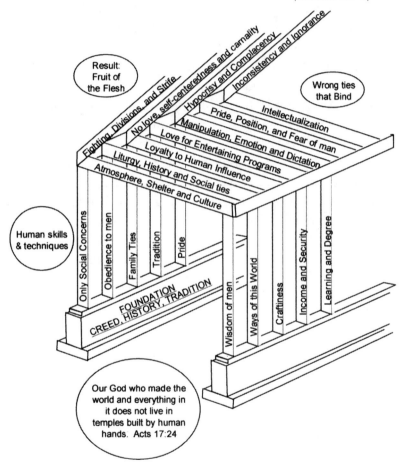

Do not conform any longer to the pattern of this world ...

(Romans 12:2)

Christ loved the church and gave Himself up for her, to mak her holy ... to present her to Himself as a radiant church, without stain or wrinkle or any blemish but holy and faultless.

(Ephesians 5:26-27)

THINK ABOUT IT!

Let's review and ask ourselves some questions:

1. Jesus never instructed us to become cathedral builders, but Kingdom seekers. He said: "I will build my Church" and instructed us: "Seek ye the Kingdom."

2. Jesus never asked us to promote His cause on earth by forming denominations or churches that run like commercial institutions.

3. Jesus had high standards for those who would follow Him. In many churches today, discipleship has been changed to "easy believism."

4. Jesus told us to be extenders of His Kingdom and commanded us to carry out the Great Commission. Many mega churches use up most of their money for their own needs with the "leftover" perhaps going to mission outreach.

5. Jesus exemplified a very simple lifestyle and so did the disciples. The Pharisees were rich "for they loved money" (Luke 16). Where did the storing up of money on earth come from?

6. Jesus wants His Spirit to be in control of the church. Biblical requirements for elders are very high in order to assure purity in the church leadership through whom the Spirit may work.

7. Jesus warned against those who are in ministry for greed and called them "hirelings." Today, ministry volunteerism in the church has become almost unknown. We have developed careerism and degrees for those in ministry. Whatever happened to the gifts and five-fold ministries of the Spirit? Are they no longer applicable today?

8. Jesus wanted His Church to be a missionary-sending church. How is it that 2,000 years after this mandate was given, we have developed many denominations and built elaborate buildings, while merely pretending we are mission-minded, using only a tiny part of the budget on missions? We have more staff to weekly entertain and cater to the folks at home than missionaries, letting the unreached millions go to eternity without

ever having heard Christ's message. Is this the church Jesus intended to build?

In light of the above, what are some of the distinguishing marks of various man-made and/or false church groups?

- They will minimize recognition of the need for salvation through a personal acceptance of Christ as our Savior. They will assume salvation or claim that there are other ways to get to heaven (John 14:6). Most of them will deny the existence of hell, claiming that God is only love and we all will be accepted or given another chance (Matthew 8:12).
- Others will deny the role of suffering, emphasizing powers of healing in accordance with their demands—thus denying the sovereignty of God or the purpose of suffering God may intend.
- Some may have powers (not from God) to do signs and wonders, much like those magicians who withstood Moses. By this, they are preparing believers for an easy acceptance of anti-Christ who will perform even greater miracles (2 Thessalonians 1:9).
- There will be those who will promote a form of spirit worship we are warned against in the Bible (Colossians 2:8).
- Most will steer away from holiness and a focus on the evidences of the fruit of the Spirit in one's life, turning instead to spiritual manifestations. These will soft peddle immorality, sin, and indulging lifestyles (2 Timothy 4:3).
- Many will blindly follow the writings and interpretations of strong leaders of the past or present, without consulting the Scriptures to ensure accuracy, (1 Corinthians 1:12; 3:4).
- Many abuse the use of God's money by refusing accountability as to how finances are disbursed and eliminating checks and balances (2 Peter 2:2).

- Presentations designed to stir up emotions and to encourage a philosophy based on "if it feels good it must be good" (2 Thessalonians 1:11).
- Being very godly in appearance, yet ignoring Christ's warning about false teachers who would come in sheep's clothing. The gift of discernment will be completely ignored by many believers (Matthew 24:24).
- Some will claim that the way to spiritual fullness does not come by refusing to live by the old nature, but merely by enlarging oneself with "spiritual experiences" and making it appear "I am holier than thou." In that way, they attempt to have the best of both worlds (Colossians 2:8).
- Minimizing the importance of biblical truth and the need to hear messages straight from God (2 Timothy 3:16).
- Warning against leaving their system, claiming they are a holy congregation, and contending that outside of their system there is no salvation.
- They seem to have forgotten that the Bible warns us that:

There is a way that seems right to a man, but in the end it leads to destruction.

(Proverbs 16:25)

PART TWO:

The Solution for the Church

Urgent Changes That Need to be Made

The following list of changes that my study of God's Word and my observation of the current North American church scene have led me to suggest are not some profound "breakthrough" insight. Basically these suggestions are simply aimed at reversing the distressing conditions now present in the church and recovering the essential biblical characteristics that are currently missing.

It really is that simple. Such changes can be accomplished *only* through the power and enabling of the Spirit of the Lord Jesus Christ, who is the Head of His Church.

May it be so, for God's glory and for blessing to us, His children, and to a needy world through our witness to the truth of the glorious gospel of Christ.

Note: The changes are not necessarily listed in order of priority.

Urgent Change # 1

Recognition of Need and Repentance

Repent and do the things you did at first.

Revelation 2:5

The Biblical Way to Repent

If my people, who are called by my name, will humble themselves and pray and seek my face and turn from their wicked ways, then will I hear from heaven and will forgive their sin and will heal their land.

(2 Chronicles 7:14)

In this passage we have God's promise for renewal and restoration, whether in our churches or in our nation. It's all based upon God's three conditions:

1. *"If my people will humble themselves"*
As a church we are often guilty because:

- We have tolerated a salvation of merely intellectual knowledge instead of living in the newness of life.
- We have turned the priesthood of all believers into a mere slogan by dividing the church into laity and clergy.
- We have allowed clergy to rule the church and, in order to survive, have turned the church into a commercial entity.
- As churches as well as believers, many have become wealthy by storing up treasures on earth causing them to have very little need of God.
- Many of us no longer look for biblical requirements in eldership, but favor those who are generous in giving and are simply in agreement with the pastor.
- We are causing division among believers as well as in the community by purporting a specific creed, thus separating ourselves from other believers and groups with whom we should have a unity in Christ.
- We no longer look for transformed lives before accepting new members, nor do we exercise church discipline with those who walk in disobedience.
- We have neglected Christ's requirements of making disciples and encouraging fruitfulness for all believers.

2. *"Pray and Seek My Face"*
Seeking God's face, first of all, is the expression of the desire to know what God requires of us as believers. We cannot pray for revival or forgiveness unless we first understand what we need to repent of and how far we have gone astray. As believers we must turn again to the Bible to know and practice what it teaches. We must pray in agreement with each other, with every intention of giving Christ His rightful place in the church, according to His desire to build His church.

How does the church become Christ's church again?

- By acknowledging that we have gone astray.
- By returning to Christ's control
- By eliminating self-sufficiency and practicing dependency.

We see this in mission agencies, with their workers who live on limited budgets from month to month. We also see this in places where the church is being persecuted and their survival and safety is totally dependent on the Lord. We must not only pray for revival, but repent and turn toward God so that He will take delight in us and have reason to respond.

> *I knew that you are a gracious and compassionate God, slow to anger and abounding in love, a God who relents from sending calamity.*
>
> (Jonah 4:2b)

3. *"Turn from Our Wicked Ways"*

It is Christ's kingship over everything in our lives and over the church that has been neglected. Some of our churches have been turned into commercial operations by making them "seeker friendly," and have compromised with the world in order to draw the youth and non-believers. This compromise is turning God's house into a consumer-entertainment center. Some groups will use attractive lectures or empty repetitious songs while others seek demonstrations of spiritual power that the Bible warns against (Colossians 2:18–19).

None of this will turn believers into disciples, but into spectators who are satisfied to simply be entertained. Others will continue to break God's laws by being tolerant of immorality, divorce, indulging lifestyles, abuse of money, and neglect of the poor and the unreached.

What are God's requirements for restoration and revival? First of all, repentance. As long as we keep on sinning, God will not hear our prayers, because He requires that we:

> *Touch not the unclean thing; and I will receive you. And will be a Father unto you, and ye shall be my sons and daughters ... Since we have these promises, dear friends, let us purify ourselves from everything that contaminates body and spirit, perfecting holiness out of reverence for God.*
>
> (2 Corinthians 6:17; 7:1)

A PRAYER FOR REVIVAL

Father, forgive us for we have sinned:

We have destroyed the divine functioning of Your Church on earth by running it upon men's ideas more than being strictly and accurately regulated by Your Word (Matthew 18:20).

We have changed the priesthood of all believers into career-priesthood for a few (1 Peter 5:2).

We have developed a hierarchy and divided Your body into clergy and laity, and only given lip service to the priesthood of all believers (1 Peter 2:4).

We have sometimes instituted church membership requirements at the expense of neglecting the standards You require of Your followers (Luke 14:26–27).

We have neglected the priority ministry of compassion from our offerings, thus limiting reaching out to the needy, the poor, and those who have never heard (1 Timothy 5:3; Ezekiel 34:1–10).

We tolerate "spiritually unemployed" believers who have become merely spectators instead of encouraging a kingdom of priests serving You together in the arena of faith (1 Peter 2:9).

We have even made idols of our denominations, severely abusing Your body, and inadvertently serving two masters (Matthew 6:24).

We have preached salvation but ignored Your instruction to make disciples by maturing the saints, who would then be spiritually productive and wholeheartedly follow You (Luke 6:46).

We have quenched Your Spirit by failing to use spiritually gifted people to serve in ministry, using that enablement with which You have blessed them (Ephesians 6:19).

We have stored up riches in our churches through properties and resources, which You told us not to do (Matthew 6:19).

We have used human exaltations that You forbade (Matthew 23:17).

We have not been promoting Your kingdom, but merely our church (Matthew 6:33).

For this and more we seek Your forgiveness and promise to repent. Amen.

May God grant that many church leaders, who should repent, *will* do so in order that this urgent need for restoration may be met.

Return to Biblical Proclamation

Preach the Word.

2 Timothy 4:2

THE MESSAGE

When Jesus sent out His followers, He gave them only one message: to preach citizenship in the kingdom of God based on repentance from sin and reconciliation to God. He gave His disciples, who proclaimed His message, power, and authority over many sicknesses and diseases (Luke 9:1–2).

Do we still need people with the prophetic attributes of *forth-telling* God's Word today? Were there such prophets among the common people in the New Testament Church?

Judas and Silas were prophets (Acts 15:32). We find three in Acts 11:27–30 and five in Acts 13:1. Yes, the church always had prophets in their midst, and it should be our prayer that many pastors will again become preachers of righteousness, boldly proclaiming God's Word, and that we will take heed to their warnings and instruction, not taking lightly their message (1 Thessalonians 5:19–21).

FORTH-TELLING PROPHETS OF THE WORD

Prophets in the Old Testament were God-inspired in *fore-telling* God's words, but with Scripture given to us we *now* have the future foretold in writing. The other role prophets had, however, was *forth-telling*, which became the preaching of repentance from unbiblical teachings or ways of living. This ministry brought Israel to repentance several times.

In one sense, New Testament prophets have an entirely different function than did those in the Old Testament, due to the fact that every Spirit-filled believer is now indwelt by the Holy Spirit and has the prophetic Word of God. There is now the biblical New Testament prophetic role of telling forth, or preaching, the Word.

Those having this ministry of prophecy must be heard. They are meant to be the watchmen and "trumpet blowers" (1 Corinthians 14:8) when they see things going in the wrong direction. The apostle Paul encouraged the gift of prophecy for all believers as a safeguard for the church to operate according to the Word of God. In 1 Corinthians 12:28 the prophet's function was of equal importance to that of the apostles.

Do we still have prophets today? Think of the great reformers, or of Jonathan Edwards, Charles Wesley, George Whitfield, C. H. Spurgeon, Charles Finney, and many others who have spoken God's Word. They were sent by God to bring the warning to repent but, like the Old Testament prophets, some were rejected.

Prophets are:

- proclaimers of truth and the need for correction and repentance.
- aiming for church restoration and reformation.
- burdened for the blindness of their people.
- many times rejected by their own church.

Prophesying is a gift we should not neglect (1 Corinthians 14:1). Prophets and their message even in our times should not be despised (1 Thessalonians 5:19–21).

Do we still need prophets today? Yes, if we, as a church, still need repentance, restoration, and renewal.

Emphasis on the Priesthood Involvement of the Believer and the Exercise of Spiritual Gifts

But you are a chosen people, a royal priesthood.
1 Peter 2:9

We have different gifts, according to the grace given us.
Romans 12:6

Apostasy sets in when people abandon the truth that saved them. In most churches we no longer hear:

- A clear call to salvation, purity, and separation
- The surrender of the old nature
- A focus on walking in the newness of life
- A financial priority for widows and orphans or going into all the world

and especially we no longer hear …

- *The call to all believers to be ministers of God*

THE PRIESTHOOD: A MINISTRY FOR ALL BELIEVERS

Even though Jesus completed the Old Testament priesthood and is called the High Priest of the New Covenant, all believers are now called to serve in a New Testament priesthood. First of all we are to minister to each other, and secondly to the world around us as beacons of light (Matthew 4:15). The Bible calls believers "a kingdom of priests" (Revelation 1:6; 5:10).

> *You also, like living stones, are being built into a spiritual house to be a holy priesthood, offering spiritual sacrifices acceptable to God through Jesus Christ.*
>
> 1 Peter 2:5

As previously stated, God has given believers the ministry of reconciliation (2 Corinthians 5:18). We are not intended to merely sit in a pew listening to a sermon and/or just supporting the system. A church was meant to be a beehive of activities with involved believers, busy in the work of their priestly ministry. *"You are a chosen people ... that you may declare the praises of him who called you out of darkness into his wonderful light"* (1 Peter 2:9).

SPIRITUAL GIFTEDNESS

> *But you will receive power when the Holy Spirit comes on you; and you will be my witnesses in Jerusalem, and in all Judea and Samaria, and to the ends of the earth.*
>
> (Acts 1:8)

Since God has given every person who has received His Spirit special gifts and abilities, His desire for us is that we use those gifts to "be fruitful and multiply." He intends that those gifts be put to effective use in building up the church and edifying other believers.

With our man-made changes in church structure, we have downplayed the importance of the enabling gifts of the Spirit in the believer's life. Thus we have caused and tolerated spiritual callousness, division, and barrenness instead of holiness and fruitfulness.

The Restoration of Biblical Eldership

*I left you in Crete ... [to] appoint elders in every town
... entrusted with God's work.*

Titus 1:5–7

CHRIST'S AUTHORITY DELEGATED

Jesus intended to rule the church through His Spirit. The question we need now to ask is, "Who is the final authority in the church today?" Is it godly elders through whom the Spirit can speak? Or do our elders merely function for a short term, being quietly eliminated when too outspoken, never to be asked to run again?

When Solomon built God's temple, the instructions were very precise. When God inspired the New Testament, the instructions therein were also very precise as to the formation and function of the church. She was to be ruled by qualified elders chosen by Divine instructions in the Word and by the Spirit, not handpicked by pastors or voted in by the whims of men.

Elders were meant to be rulers in the church and to be equal in relation to each other. Every ministry in the church was to be led by men who are able to hear the voice of the Spirit and not be guided by human wisdom. They were to lead, plan, and move *"as the Spirit directed them."*

ELDERS: MINISTRY OF SHEPHERDING

Here is an Old Testament ministry Jesus gave to His new church—the ministry of shepherding. There is a serious error in the church today: elders are not chosen by biblical requirements and are not required to operate according to scriptural practices. A church is not a church unless it has a team of elders who meet God's requirements. Elders were meant to be key to the church as God-fearing men who are gifted and able to be the leaders. It was with the appointment of elders that the gathering of believers became a church (Acts 14:23; Titus 5:1).

Timothy and Titus gave us the description for eldership and were the first to appoint elders in the new churches (Titus 1:5). When the apostles wrote letters or contacted the churches they always addressed the elders (Acts 20:17). Elders in both the Old and New Testament were carefully chosen and ordained for duty (Acts 14:23) and functioned as long as they were able to serve.

REQUIREMENTS FOR ELDERS

The health of a church stands or falls with the spiritual calibre of the elders a church has chosen. Biblical eldership was not just an honorary position for people who agree with anything the pastor would suggest or who have a blind loyalty to the denomination.

All leadership of a biblical church come forth from a plurality of elders. Whether pastor or evangelist, regardless of their function, these were always considered fellow elders, with no higher authority or ranking (1 Peter 5:1).

- Elders, as the name indicates, were older men who had a mature, close relationship with God, and who were established in the Word and life experience.
- Elders were meant to be ordained (Acts 14:23). This requirement being only for eldership meant that they were to be permanent in the church.
- Elders were meant to be as examples to the flock, and form the leadership team of the church by being involved in ministry in whatever enablement the Spirit may have given them.
- Elders could have a variety of ministry gifts such as pastoring, teaching, healing, prophesying, leading, administrating, evangelizing, and any other gift the Lord may have given them for the functioning of the church and the building up of believers in the faith.
- Elders were to be *"men from among you who are known to be full of the Spirit and wisdom"* (Acts 6:3). It is through these men the Lord wants to speak and lead the church and its ministries.

Because of the highly influential position we have given to pastors, many churches no longer see the need for and function of true biblical elders and they have been reduced to board members of a man-made system. The Bible encourages believers to be willing to serve as elders but has high standards for this office. Let's look at what these requirements really are as explained in 1 Timothy 3:2–7, Titus 1:6–8, and 1 Peter 5:1–5.

Above Reproach. Elders are meant to be chosen from those who are exemplary in character, both in their occupation and in their church life. Other passages describe them as blameless, not domineering, but revealing abundantly the fruit of the Spirit, such as love, humility, patience, self-control, goodness, faithfulness, and kindness.

Having One Wife. This qualification relates to the moral purity of the individual, the spiritual stability of the husband/wife relationship, and his adherence to the teaching of Scripture about marriage.

Temperate in disposition. An elder must be gentle in handling situations, showing godly wisdom, and refusing to come to biased conclusions.

Self-Controlled. A truly Spirit-controlled person is a self-controlled person. The Bible says clearly *"he who controls his own temper [is stronger] than one who takes a city"* (Proverbs 16:32).

Respectable. This speaks of orderliness, trustworthiness, and being exemplarily in lifestyle. The apostle Paul illustrated this when he challenged believers to follow him as he would follow Christ (2 Thessalonians 3:7).

Hospitable. The early church met often in homes and the elder's ministry was to begin from his home. Together with his wife, he is to show concern to those who have needs, and have the ability to minister to these.

Able to Teach. An elder must know the Word and be able to serve in the pulpit or teach others. This does not mean he must do it alone. Spiritual ministries always came in multiples of people, and ministry was never meant to be a one-man endeavour.

No Drunkenness. Even though wine was a very common drink in New Testament times, this verse speaks of addiction and over-indulgence. A Christian leader should be an example and be God-controlled in all aspects of life.

Not Violent. A spirit-controlled person is not a violent person and not a self-seeker, but one who can put the interests of others before his own. He tolerates other insights or opinions and does not promote a private interpretation of Scripture.

Not Quarrelsome. All too often, a Bible study can turn into a debate. People who are effective leaders do not become quarrelsome but encourage others to share their views on Scripture.

No Lover of Money. The early church was discouraged from hiring leaders who were money-motivated and who simply looked at ministry as a job. Jesus instructed His followers to freely give as they had freely received the gospel (Matthew 10:8). The apostle Paul also spoke of not wanting to be a burden to anyone who was not able to give, and at many times he was self-supporting (2 Corinthians 11:7–9). We, however, live in an age of materialism and our present system has prevented many churches from properly helping those whom the Bible commands a church to care for. An elder is not to be centered on money but on the things of God.

Exemplary Family. *"If anyone does not know how to manage his own family, how can he take care of God's people?"* (1 Timothy 3:5). My wife and I once were invited to a home fellowship group. After attending for a few months we became aware that the teacher and his wife's children were not walking with the Lord, but instead were living most unruly lives. I will never forget the disappointment that fell over the group and how ineffective his ministry became after this was revealed. An elder must be able to wisely lead his family.

No Recent Convert. People will sometimes put young men or a recent convert on a pedestal. How dangerous it can be when spiritually immature people jump into leadership. This often leads to pride instead of soundness in the Word and having direction from God. An elder is to be mature in the faith.

A Good Rapport. Another qualification for eldership relates to one's rapport with the outside world. Claiming to be a Christian but not having an honest lifestyle and not being well spoken of by business associates can often do enormous harm to the name of Christ. Elders who work in the commercial world know there is sometimes a cost attached to be known as a

Christian and that they must always show a forgiving and humble attitude.

Small Groups led by truly biblically qualified elders who know the Word are the key to healthy growth for many believers as well as for the church. The Bible sets a high standard, with explicit qualifications for these men. We, in return, must have deep respect towards them.

> *Obey your leaders and submit to their authority. They keep watch over you as men who must give an account. Obey them so that their work will be a joy, not a burden, for that would be of no advantage to you.*
>
> (Hebrews 13:17)

These requirements do not mean we look for perfection as a qualification for leadership. As believers we know our perfection is only in Christ, but the fruit of the Spirit must be seen in the walk and temperament of those whom we ask to serve and direct the church, whether as a teaching elder or in leading other functions or ministries.

The rewards for faithful, biblical elders are set forth in Scripture:

> *To the elders among you, I appeal as a fellow elder, a witness of Christ's sufferings and one who also will share in the glory to be revealed. Be shepherds of God's flock that is under your care, serving as overseers—not because you must, but because you are willing, as God wants you to be; not greedy for money, but eager to serve; not lording it over those entrusted to you, but being examples to the flock. And when the Chief Shepherd appears, you will receive the crown of glory that will never fade away.*
>
> (1 Peter 5:1–4)

But what if a church feels that they have no one willing or desiring to serve in eldership? Or what if a church ignores all the requirements for biblical eldership? The apostle Paul even writes that those willing to serve as an overseer desire a good thing (1 Timothy 3:1).

If a church fails in proper eldership, she will also have failed the Lord in other areas of obedience. And in these cases, the options are either for the church to repent or for individuals to find another place of fellowship.

LEADERSHIP IN THE CHURCH

Elders, whose proper function and biblical requirements have already been discussed, are minimized or done away with in many churches. They were meant to be leaders in the church; even the senior pastor is to be an elder with the gift of expounding the Scripture. He was never meant to rule the church or to be the CEO, but a servant leader and a fellow shepherd.

A return to biblical eldership is an urgent need if Christ is to be the Head of the Church as it was intended it to be. This must begin with spiritually transformed and Holy Spirit-equipped believers who desire to do God's work in God's way. Gathering places should be simple in design, practical and economical in usefulness. Elders must exemplify their faith in a biblical lifestyle and humility. Pastoral elders must be those who do not seek power or desire to have final authority, but who are compassionate servant leaders.

A plurality of leadership under Christ's control is needed with all the ministries of the church, with the Spirit being at work within and throughout the body. Wouldn't it be great if we could be a church of Christ's design, with the ministries Christ intended the church to have and with the Lord being supernaturally at work in our midst?

A biblical eldership is not only an essential part of such a church, it is a must.

Stimulation of Love, Fellowship and Practical Concern within the Body

Since God so loved us, we also ought to love one another.
1 John 4:11

The Bible gives us a long list of "relational commandments" such as loving, caring, praying, encouraging, and standing in for each other. The Christian life was never meant to be a life of individualism, but was intended by God to be a caring community. That's the way it was at the beginning of the church.

The New Testament believers met even during the week to fellowship, minister, and pray. They were also helping, caring, and encouraging each other in physical as well as spiritual ways. As the world saw how much the early Christians loved each other, some even sold their possessions in order to help those who had needs; many, even thousands, were drawn to the Christian faith as a result.

GOD CARES ABOUT HUMAN NEED AND SO SHOULD WE

God wants us to take double care of those in need.

> *Religion that God our Father accepts as pure and faultless is this: to look after orphans and widows in their distress and to keep oneself from being polluted by the world.*
>
> (James 1:27)

God is pleased when in the disbursement of funds we remember the needy.

> *There will always be poor people in the land. Therefore I command you to be openhanded toward your brothers and toward the poor and needy in your land.*
>
> (Deuteronomy 15:11)

> *All they asked was that we should continue to remember the poor, the very thing I was eager to do.*
>
> (Galatians 2:10)

God commands you, as a believer, to open wide your hand to your brother, the needy, and the poor.

> *If anyone has material possessions and sees his brother in need but has no pity on him, how can the love of God be in him? ... Let us not love with words or tongue but with actions and in truth.*
>
> (1 John 3:17–18)

And who are needier than those who have never heard the gospel?

> *Therefore go and make disciples of all nations, baptizing*
> *them in the name of the Father and of the Son and of the*
> *Holy Spirit, and teaching them to obey everything I have*
> *commanded you. And surely I am with you always, to the*
> *very end of the age.*
>
> (Matthew 28:19, 20)

God wants us to minister to the physical as well as the spiritual needs.

> *Suppose you see a brother or sister who has no food or*
> *clothing, and you say, "Good-bye and have a good day;*
> *stay warm and eat well"—but then you don't give that*
> *person any food or clothing. What good does that do?*
>
> (James 2:15–16 NLT)

In the Bible we have fifty-nine commands concerning things we should do unto and for each other as we come together as believers. We should encourage, care, love, confess, pray, minister, restore, and a lot more.

I made up a list of all these "do unto others" commands and took this list to church. I was shocked to realize that we did almost none of these in our traditional services.

Obviously, we urgently need to get back to demonstrating practical love to one another as well as making time to fellowship in the Lord, and thus build up one another.

URGENT NEED # 6

Focus on Evangelism and Missions

Do the work of an evangelist.
2 Timothy 4:5

You will be my witnesses ... to the ends of the earth.
Acts 1:8

Today in many churches we have comfortable gathering centers, good entertainment, and a "seeker friendly" atmosphere. We sometimes seek the spectacular spiritual gifts more than we seek the Giver.

Many churches have thus become "kingdoms of men" rather than centers that demonstrate a total commitment to the kingdom of God. Unfortunately, in the midst of all this our passion is no longer caring for the widows, orphans, single moms, or the millions who have never heard the Gospel. Well over ninety percent of most church budgets are spent to keep the internal system going.

Something we previously suggested bears repeating at this point. Jesus wanted His Church to be a missionary church. How is it that two thousand years after this mandate we have developed many denominations, built elaborate buildings, pretending that we are mission-minded, but use only a tiny part of our budgets on missions? As said before we sometimes have more staff to weekly entertain and cater to the folks at home than we have missionaries. We have let the unreached millions go to eternity without ever having heard Christ's message. Is this the church Jesus intended to build?

Sadly, the church in many places is more focused on seeing people placed under their authority than on being a force under God's Authority of strong individuals who want to reach the world for Christ.

EXTENDING CHRIST'S KINGDOM

Everyone looks out for his own interests, not those of Jesus Christ.

(Philippians 2:21)

Jesus did not come to offer His followers a religious franchise or to make a career for them. He wanted them to proclaim His message of being able to enter into His kingdom and, through a new relationship with Him, to be delivered from the ways and methods of this world.

Yet the opposite has taken place. We are now using earthly marketing methods and ranks of command in promoting religious concepts, institutionalized religion, and a man-created religious system based on our own interpretation of the Bible.

Church activities are not necessarily kingdom activities. Many Christians and churches do very little to bring others into the Christian faith and do not extend the kingdom of God because of self-preoccupation or a lack of confidence. To have only self- or social concerns shows we have lost sight of God's kingdom's growth and are merely seeking our own. God's kingdom only grows when people become passionately filled with Christ's love for others.

Yes, praise God, there are still churches today that, from the top down, are based on volunteers who are committed to fulfilling the Lord's desires. It is in such churches that needs are being met, growth is continuous, and resources are being wisely used to send forth laborers into the field. The field is always the world, not the church, and the church therefore should work with a minimal overhead, not being focused on itself, but being intent on the training and development of believers for outreach, using most of its resources to do evangelism and missions.

Why is Money Such an Issue?

As believers, our call is to spiritual fruitfulness in the propagation of the gospel. This has a lot to do with how we handle our money. The wrong use or withholding of what could otherwise be invested in the Lord's work in outreach is like withholding the gospel from those who are spiritually poor having never heard that message.

Jesus warned us not to make his Father's house a place of merchandise. We, in return, have neglected God's supply of spiritually gifted believers who would gladly volunteer for various forms of ministry, but turned the organized church into an employment center, and taken sacrifice out of ministry.

Commercialized religion has turned pastors into CEOs, made worship into entertainment and brought into the church unbiblical money-raising methods. This has also deprived many believers of the joy of giving.

Money is a major issue for the spiritual health of the believer as well as the church. The right use of money given to the Lord will bless the believer as well as the church. It will cause a greater global outreach as well as provide care to those who have financial needs.

Because of the large amount of money needed, many churches face shortages even with large amounts of money coming in. Of the early church, we read that she reached out to the needy and that *"there was no needy people among them"* (Acts 4:34). Because of wrong priorities and disbursements, many churches today merely exist to feed their own system while ignoring other needs. Having exchanged spiritually-gifted voluntary leadership for paid servants, we have further reduced our ability to help the needy or to support missionary ministries.

MANDATE IGNORED

Jesus gave us a mandate to care for the needy and go into all the world with His message. The church today has, for the most part, ignored that mandate and treats missions and benevolence as an added option instead of the reason for its existence. The Bible speaks clearly regarding the mandate of the church, but we have chosen our own priorities.

One of the sad results of this disobedience is that the church suffers. It is a well-documented fact that churches that have a strong missions/evangelism program experience growth and have fewer problems in meeting their budgets than churches that don't have that emphasis. We should not be surprised at this, for when we obey God, we experience His blessing.

Therefore, for the good of the church, for blessing to the needy world and for joy in the lives of believers, an urgent need is the recovery of a strong focus on evangelism, Christ-centered social concerns, and world missions.

URGENT NEED # 7

Small-group Ministry

Greet also the church that meets at their house.

Romans 16:5

REFRESHING CLOSENESS

It is very refreshing to come together as believers in a small gathering and find a common oneness, not primarily in dogma nor in creed but in Jesus Himself. He promised where two or three are gathered in His Name, He would be present (Matthew 18:20). Christ's presence creates unity and love in these groups, because we are no longer dogma-focused but God-focused and centered.

HOME GROUPS

*Where two or three come together in my name, there am
I with them.*

(Matthew 18:20)

Thankfully, there are varieties of groups using names such as accountability groups, fellowship groups or, as they are called in the Bible, *"the church that meets at your house"* (Romans 16:3; 1 Corinthians 16:19; Colossians 4:15; Philippians 1:2).

Small groups are every bit as much a "church" as are our larger gatherings. Jesus said where even two or three are meeting in His name, He will be there in the midst of them. Many groups may not even have a name; they just simply meet in Jesus' name! In China, despite persecution, these home groups now comprise the largest and fastest growing church in the world.

We may not be able to quickly change some of the structure of a church, but we can do a lot through small groups. Another reason small group gatherings are important is that a time may come when you will find it very disturbing to go to church. Some preachers may no longer proclaim the Word of God, thus putting more and more people to sleep spiritually.

CAN WE BECOME CHRIST'S CHURCH AGAIN?

Over the years we have enjoyed a small taste of this biblical way of gathering and experiencing the presence of the Lord as we became involved in small groups. I even had the opportunity to serve as volunteer staff member in charge of the small group ministry in the First Baptist Church of Calgary, Alberta. The Spirit of God met many needs in those gatherings. The meetings were spontaneous, internal, supernatural, people-focused, and beneficial. No one looked at the clock. We shared and cared for each other. We built each other up in faith and usefulness for the Lord.

But will we ever meet in such a manner again? Yes, we can:

- when Christians meet in an informal and open atmosphere.
- when meetings are no longer program-, man-, church- or time-controlled.
- when Jesus' presence can be felt and seen through answered prayer.
- when testimonies and praise can be freely expressed.
- when we become desperate enough to want a change, and
- when people have time to share openly, to love, care and pray for each other.

Have you noticed how often in the Bible Jesus ate with people while on earth? Sharing food with one another and having discussion around a table can break many barriers. Suddenly there is openness and we have all the time that is needed.

SMALL GROUP BENEFITS

Many Churches of Today:	*Early Church or Small Group:*
Unnatural form of gathering	Enthusiastic coming together
Costly to operate	Run by volunteers
Lacks relationship	Stimulates participation
Uncomfortable to attend	Unforgettable gatherings
Focused on numbers	Focused on each other
Lecture oriented	Sharing based
Obligated to attend	Eagerly attended
Doctrinally restricted	Jesus is the unifying factor

Which form of meeting would you prefer?

CONSIDERATIONS FOR SMALL GROUP MINISTRY

Having been involved in small groups for many years it did not take long for us to discover that many churches discourage groups they cannot control. However, when groups become controlled by men's agendas, there is little room left for openness and spontaneity.

A small group should have the freedom of the Spirit so people can express their hearts, expressing struggles or issues, to bring each other into a deeper and fuller relationship with Jesus Christ. The following are some of the characteristics small group leaders should display.

BIBLICAL LEADERSHIP

Church elders who meet the biblical description of eldership can be great leaders in small groups even simply by being examples to the flock. Each small group can be as much a church as the church itself and could become a real blessing to the spiritual development of the larger church. The small group movement could result in renewal for the church or at least provide great spiritual growth, encouragement, and blessing to the participants.

OPEN TO ALL

As previously mentioned, mixing people from other backgrounds into a group can be most refreshing. Exchanging insights should be permitted, provided we have unity in Christ. If it weren't for the Baptists, I would never have learned about believers' baptism; the Nazarenes taught me a lot about the importance of holiness; the Mennonites made me considerably less militaristic; and my dear Pentecostal friends brought back a renewed emphasis on the Holy Spirit. This list could go on but what do we all have in common? Jesus!

If Jesus is truly our central focus, other differences will be easily tolerated and will become small. To have the Holy Spirit in you but be locked up by tradition and formality is like having a tiger in a cage. When your identity is in Christ, you will have a desire to share Him with others.

So many church people think, "If we believe right then we must be right." But just believing right is not enough (James 2:19). We must actually be born of God. Many even take this new birth for granted. It is not what we know, but Whom we know, that brings salvation.

GIVING UP TIME AND TRADITION

Everyone who has left ... for my sake will receive a hundred times as much.

(Matthew 19:29)

Small groups meeting in homes were the model of the early church. We have become so busy with ourselves—whether in making money, enjoying pleasures, or solving problems—that we have little concern or time for others. We feel going to church is all we need. But the question is, "Is God satisfied with that?" A song I heard many years ago goes like this:

"I am satisfied, I am satisfied with Jesus.
But the question comes to me as I think of Calvary
'Is my Savior satisfied with me?'"

Each of us as a Christian is meant to be an instrument for God. It is only when we make ourselves available to Him that our problems will look small and we will find more meaning and purpose in life. Remember the words of Jesus: *"It is more blessed to give than to receive"* (Acts 20:35).

Unfortunately, in a time when everyone is so busy with

themselves, there seems to be an unwillingness to open our homes and show love for others. Many Christians are living in loneliness and isolation because they have never been brought to spiritual maturity; many times they have had no opportunity to open up to others.

The Christian life was never meant to be lived out alone nor should it be a "matter of survival of the fittest." Each of us needs encouragement to run our race for Christ. By helping and caring for each other we begin to function in accordance with Christ's design and become abundantly blessed ourselves.

You don't have to be a great teacher to start a small group. Simply open your home and pour some coffee, and you will see the various "gifts of help" come into action as God provides. It is with the opening of yourself and your home that it all begins.

LIVING FOR PLEASURE

But [she] who lives for pleasure is dead even while she lives.

(1 Timothy 5:6)

If we become engrossed and fall in love with the physical and material things in life that will never satisfy, we will soon lose sight of the things of God. The Bible challenges us this way: *"So we fix our eyes not on what is seen, but on what is unseen. For what is seen is temporary, but what is unseen is eternal"* (2 Corinthians 4:18).

Christianity is not really a religion but is primarily a transforming power, a relationship, and a life to be lived. Jesus did not merely come to save us from the consequences of sin but to use us to serve Him as our King. Therefore, our focus must be on living for Him. To be His disciples may involve giving up a lot of things and reaching out to others who are stuck either in the world or in a religious system that enslaves and keeps them in darkness. This is what our Christian calling is all about.

Do It Now

Whoever turns a sinner from the error of his way will save him from death and cover over a multitude of sins.

(James 5:20)

God can use each of us in our own sphere to become agents for him. But the question is, are we willing to open our homes and take the time to meet with others for this purpose? Or do we think one church service per week is all that is required of us or that God cannot use us?

Are we willing to humble ourselves and speak to others about things that are most important in life? Are we willing to open up our hearts to others so they may know what Christ means to us and find more meaning in Him as well?

Everything in life begins with a decision of the will. It was Jesus who throughout His life prayed, "Father, not mine but Your will be done." It is when we sincerely say the same that God will use us.

You Will Be Blessed

Whatever you did for one of the least of these brothers of mine, you did for me.

(Matthew 25:40)

Throughout the years we have had all kinds of small groups in our home. Some groups were focused on new believers, while others were an outreach to unbelievers. Most of all, we were focused on seeing believers become mature disciples in the Lord. Broken lives were restored. Street people became productive citizens. The abused were given help and healing.

One pastor even said, "I have seen more people restored in your living room than in many a church." A new believer uttered during a meeting, "I think Jesus is here because of answered prayer." Yes, Jesus was at those meetings, with attendance usually from eight to twenty-four people. We met weekly for up to two years, and then each one was encouraged to start a group with others. These gatherings also helped us find more meaning, purpose, and much joy in life, instead of just living for self or merely going to church.

A NEW RELATIONSHIP

We would like to see Jesus.

(John 12:21)

Jesus invited His followers, whoever they were, rich or poor, black or white, to come together and meet around Him—not around a piece of paper with a statement or creed.

People who have experienced meeting exclusively around Jesus only, be it in homes, concentration or army camps or in jails, will state this was the greatest form of fellowship they ever had. They learned to encourage and love each other, to bear each others' burdens, pray fervently for each other, and continue to be devoted to each other.

LIFTING UP JESUS

When I am lifted up from the earth, [I] will draw all men to myself.

(John 12:32)

When we realize what Jesus requires of us, we become compassionate and caring for each other. Then, we will try to carry each others' burdens and confess our faults one to another. We won't judge each other, but we will teach, encourage, and spur each other on to doing better and better in our spiritual walks.

Being hospitable and caring for each other is a duty Jesus requests of us. This is what gathering around Him is all about.

Let us hold unswervingly to the hope we profess, for he who promised is faithful. And let us consider how we may spur one another on toward love and good deeds. Let us not give up meeting together, as some are in the habit of doing, but let us encourage one another—and all the more as you see the Day approaching.

(Hebrews 10:23–24)

This Bible passage offers three vital suggestions:

1. *"Do not give up coming together as believers."* Many churches have become a mixture of believers and unbelievers and are no longer "a gathering of believers" or much of a light in our present darkness.

2. *"Let us encourage one another."* Our spiritual food should not come from one person; rather we are commanded to encourage *one another* to be steadfast and strong in the Lord. There are fifty-nine relational commandments in the Bible on what we should do for each other, like encouraging, praying, loving, correcting, and teaching. For the most part we are not doing this in our meetings; therefore we must come together in small groups as believers.

3. *"Especially as you see the Day approaching."* The New Testament Church began as house groups. We would do well to start meeting again in small groups. Every believer has spiritual gifts and a duty to help protect and warn others concerning the rapid decay around us. Thus we will be prepared for dangerous times and be able to stand to the end, even if the church may have failed us.

In later times some will abandon the faith and follow deceiving spirits and things taught by demons.

(1 Timothy 4:1)

Without question, for revival and survival, the small group ministry in the local church is of vital importance.

A House Built By God

What would the church that Jesus intended us to have be like? Ephesians chapter two gives us the facts:

- Vs. 8: For it is by grace that you have been saved, through faith—and this is not from yourselves, it is the gift of God
- Vs. 10: For we are God's workmanship, created to be light in the world.
- Vs. 11: Formerly we were not, but now we are born of his Spirit.
- Vs. 12: At one time we were without hope but Christ

133

became our rescuer.

- Vs. 19: Now we are part of a house designed by Christ,
- Vs. 20: Built on the foundation of the apostles and the prophets,
- Vs. 20: With Jesus Christ as the cornerstone of it all.
- Vs. 21: We are framed together to become a temple for our Lord.
- Vs. 22: And have become a dwelling place for him on earth.

THE LOCAL CHURCH—BUILT BY CHRIST'S DESIGN

Now concerning spiritual gifts ... I would not have you ignorant.
(1 Cor 12:1)

FACTS:
Eph 2 :10 The Church is the workmanship of Christ
:11 Formerly we were far off
:12 Excluded from the covenants and kingdom
:19 Now parts of the house
:20 Jesus is the Foundation
:21 We are fitly framed together
:22 Forming a habitation of God!

Rom 12
1 Cor 12
Eph 4

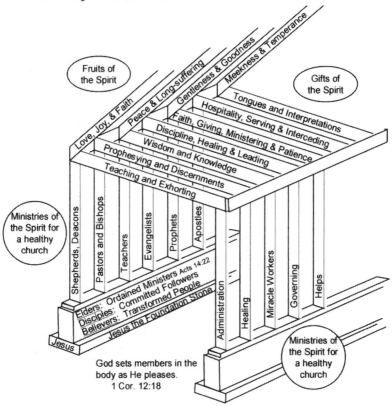

God sets members in the
body as He pleases.
1 Cor. 12:18

For the perfecting of the believers
For the perpetuation of the ministries
For the effectiveness of the Body (Church)
Eph. 4:12

135

THE FOUNDATION IS JESUS

Let us remember that men cannot build a living church. The Bible clearly tells us that our God, who made the world and everything in it, does not live in a temple made by human hands (Acts 17:24). If one wants to become a follower of Christ, he must be born of God's Spirit. It is from living stones assembled together that Jesus forms His Church.

We cannot base a church on merely a statement of faith, a common culture or traditions, but only upon our spiritual unity as people who have been born into Jesus. *"For no one can lay any foundation other than the one already laid, which is Jesus Christ"* (1 Corinthians 3:11).

The church was not made known to previous generations. It is a continuation of God's love towards the human race. It is a mystery revealed by the Spirit of Christ to the prophets of old and the twelve apostles (Ephesians 3:5).

ITS PURPOSE

The church is made up of true believers in whom God dwells. The church is also God's dwelling place as believers come together to worship Him and:

> *To prepare God's people for works of service, so that the body of Christ may be built up until we all reach unity in the faith and in the knowledge of the Son of God and become mature, attaining to the whole measure of the fullness of Christ.*
> (Ephesians 4:12–13, also 1 Corinthians 12:28)

To say that the ministries and the gifts of the Spirit are not for today is perhaps the cause of the many man-made churches. To say apostles of the church are not mentioned in the Bible is untrue. To say the role of the prophets has come to an end is denying what the apostle Paul wrote—if we desire any gift it should be correction, which should be done by the prophets among us (1 Corinthians 14:1, 5, 39)!

Instead of depending on the ministries of the Spirit, many churches are based on the interpretation of the Bible contained in earlier writings or creeds written by their forefathers, leaving little room for freedom to have other insights or interpretations.

Others have taken away the authority from God and are controlled by men, having also little room for a prophet's voice for change.

This is what a great scholar wrote:

"In essentials Unity
In non essentials Liberty
In all things Charity."

The freedom for Christ's Spirit to work through people makes the difference. Those who try to build a church in the flesh using human design and regulations are carnally minded and cannot please God (Romans 8:5–8).

THE JOISTS OR BEAMS—GIFTS OF THE SPIRIT

We have different gifts, according to the grace given to us. If a man's gift is prophesying, let him use it ... If it is serving, let him serve; if it is teaching, let him teach; if it is encouraging, let him encourage; if it is contributing to the needs of others, let him give generously; if it is leadership, let him govern diligently; if it is showing mercy, let him do it cheerfully.

(Romans 12:6–8)

Here are the ties that bind the walls together and form the ceiling in the house.

"Let each person function in whatever area God has gifted them." This was the intention of our Lord. The basic ties that bind a man-made church together are great preaching, socials, loyalty, pet doctrines, pride, and the fear of leaving.

In a church built by God, however, there is fellowship, unity, and freedom to participate; for *"where the Spirit of the Lord is there is liberty."* It is only when there is spiritual freedom in the church, where members can participate as they feel led, that the body begins to function properly.

> *Consequently, you are no longer foreigners and aliens, but fellow citizens with God's people and members of God's household, ... In him the whole building is joined together and rises to become a holy temple in the Lord.*
> (Ephesians 2:19,21)

THE RAFTERS—THE FRUIT OF THE SPIRIT

The results of a man-made church are often lack of love, coldness, self-centeredness, disunity, and church splits. The fruit of the Spirit in the church that Christ designed is love, joy, peace, patience, kindness, goodness, faithfulness, gentleness, and self-control (Galatians 5:22). Spirit-controlled people will care for others.

The fruit of the Spirit reveals who we really are and whether or not we have truly died to the flesh in order to be alive in Christ. Those who function in the flesh cannot please God and are also lacking in spiritual enthusiasm.

Solidity in faith will lead to unity and productivity among believers. A church built by Christ's design will begin with elders who meet biblical requirements and are open to whatever function God assigns them in the church.

The Alternative Church

The question many people have is "What should a truly biblical church look like?" The answer could be very elaborate, let's look at a few aspects:

And what will hold the church together?

The Walls—Ministries of the Spirit

And in the church God has appointed first of all apostles, second prophets, third teachers, then workers of miracles, also those having gifts of healing, those able to help others, those with the gifts of administration, and those speaking in different kinds of tongues.

(1 Corinthians 12:28)

Structure

In the business world, leadership means having authority. The kingdom concept, however, is opposite, "Those who want to be great must be servants" (Matthew 23:11, paraphrased). Consider this concept in diagram form.

How Do You View the Church?

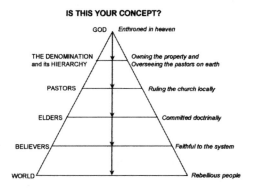

IS THIS YOUR CONCEPT?

139

The church was meant to be there for the people, but we seemingly use the people to be there for the church. The main purpose of the church, as individual believers or as a body, is to extend the kingdom of God. Therefore our focus should be "the world" as seen on the second diagram and especially those who have never heard.

It is the world Christ loved and for whom He died.
It is the believers' challenge to bring the world to Christ.
It is the elders who serve the believers.
It is the five-fold ministry of the Spirit that leads the church.
It is God who, through the Spirit, enables these ministries.

Whoever wants to become great among you must be your servant ... For even the Son of Man did not come to be served, but to serve.

(Mark 10:43, 45)

CONTROL

The church God honors is a church that is controlled by His Spirit and not manipulated by men. When God truly controls a church, the Holy Spirit's presence is very evident. In such a church the elders are godly men, living up to biblical requirements. Leadership with a multiplicity of spiritual gifts is very obvious, and the church's primary concern is the growth and care for the Body.

FINANCES AND FOCUS

People give out of love and not by human motivation or legislation. Many ministries that serve are, as much as possible, self-supporting and do not operate mainly upon the "hireling basis." The misuse of money is limited to the proper functioning of the church and its ministry.

The focus of our giving should be the needy among us and reaching out to those who have never heard. Missions money should be used for the support of exemplary mission workers in many different agencies that are among us today, not only to extend our own denomination.

OBJECTIVE

The objective of a church should not be to establish a name for itself nor store up riches or big assets on earth, but to be a useful tool for the extension of God's kingdom.

To reiterate, this should be done first of all by developing and training believers into spiritual maturity and ministry. Second, it is done by helping and loving the needy among us, to which we are admonished throughout the Bible, so our actions will speak louder than our words. Third, it is done by cautiously using God's money so there will be plenty available to reach out to those who have not yet heard.

The passion, the goal, and the object is to glorify the Lord by not conforming to the ways and mindset of this world, but instead being a supernatural beacon of light for Him in this darkened world.

CHRIST'S INTENDED CHURCH

Let us summarize what Jesus intended the church to look like.

- **Christ's church** cannot be just a man-made organization. More than anything else it is a divine institution, distinctive in admission and deliberate in the purpose of enlarging Christ's kingdom, not its own.
- **Christ's church** is universally the same. It is not formed simply around an intellectual creed but is formed around the Word of God. People are miraculously transformed into believers through Christ's atoning sacrifice.
- **Christ's church** requires of its participants a new birth, an obedient walk and a measuring up to biblical requirements for leadership. No human admission requirements may be added to what Christ has given us.
- **Christ's church** is foremost a mystical body into which believers are welcomed and encouraged to function according to their giftedness. There should be no such thing as inactive pew-warming member.
- **Christ's church** was never meant to be a spectator movement where a few ministers perform, but rather a beehive of action in which all voluntarily and enthusiastically serve the King.
- **Christ's church** was not primarily a lecturing forum but a relational movement where all believers minister to each other. Present church structure has the tendency to minimize this concept.
- **Christ's church** believers may not fully understand all Scripture but have received Christ's Spirit and are engaged in living out Christ's teachings in whatever way God has enabled them.
- **Christ's church** has always been hated by this world

142

because its members are not of this world and refuse to conform to the way, wisdom, structure, and methods of this world.

- **Christ's church** as a ministering body will also reach out to the needs around them—the orphans, widows, and the poor. It's a restoration movement having an ultimate goal of restoring struggling people both at home and abroad to a functional and useful relationship to God.

For further review of the divinely designed church, note:

A BIBLICAL FORMAT

- A biblical form of gathering, as Christ intended, will build up believers, equip them for service, and help them to live out the Christian life. It will increase prayer and love for each other, strengthen the unity of the body, and prevent a falling away of believers.
- A biblical church is a family in which the members care for one another, a body that functions correctly as all parts are in use. God's Church was meant to be a house where each piece of building material is connected and each is esteeming the others in love.
- A biblical church is Christ-controlled. Human-control will only create a man-made church that will easily fall because it causes a continual division. Human controlled churches often present salvation in a very shallow manner. Scripture can easily be inappropriately used when it lacks examination by the body. God's spiritual provisions for a restored and a better functioning church require His designed control.
- A biblical church is a vibrant church. It is a place where believers love each other and the Holy Spirit is miracu-

lously at work in its midst. This is the church that Jesus intended for us to have. It is still possible today. However, for this to happen we cannot function by man's design. Otherwise, further decay and persecution is sure to come. This might be God's judgment upon the church.

OUR POTENTIAL

"If you love me, obey my commandments," Jesus says. This includes forming and being a church that is in accordance with His design. The results of being used by God are indescribable.

Can you imagine:
- a church that is bursting with people who are involved?
- a church that is continually preparing people for service?
- a church that doesn't worry about itself but is doing Christ's work?
- a church that is fully based on ministries of the Spirit?
- a church where leaders are spiritually equipped and motivated to serve?
- a church that is spending most of its funds on outreach?
- a church that is a place of excitement with care and love for each other?

This is the church that Jesus intended us to be, and it is within our reach if we are willing to turn in repentance to the Lord and ask for His help and guidance toward change.

God is not willing that people should perish nor is He happy with churches that are not under His control or formed according to His design. The church in the West has become stagnant and in many places merely exists for its own benefit. Christians are sometimes led to believe that attending, joining, and giving to a church is good enough, but fewer and fewer people are finding joy and satisfaction in this.

Our own actions have brought the church into this deterio-
rated shape, but it can also be through our God-directed actions
that a change can be achieved.

Consider the following list of biblical requirements that came
to me some time ago.

BIBLICAL CHURCH REQUIREMENTS

1. Unconditional faith in Jesus Christ and obedience to all His
    teachings as to the spiritual requirements as revealed in
    Scripture (1 John 14:15).
2. Constant, continual communication with God through
    prayer for the Lord's direction through its leaders (1 Peter
    2:23).
3. Biblical standards for elders and believers (1 Timothy 3:1–13,
    Titus 1:5–9).
4. Plural or shared pastoral leadership within each congregation
    (Acts 14:23).
5. Decision-making by Spirit-guided consensus in the church
    and home.
6. Seeing the Christian ministry in the diversity of gifts given to
    all believers (1 Corinthians 12:4–7, 1 Peter 2:4–9).
7. Seeing the principal task of the church to be maturing the
    believers, appointing and equipping them for ministry based
    upon their giftedness and willingness to serve (Ephesians 4:12).
8. A preferential financial concern for the poor and single or
    widowed mothers in the church's life, ministry, and budget
    (James 1:26–27).
9. Grounding the church's life and theology in real Christian
    community, with a balance in self-service, community, and
    witness (Colossians 2:8, 20).
10. Small group structures for spiritual growth and healing that
    will lead to commitment and belief translated into becoming
    doers of the Word (Hebrews 3:13; 10:24–25).

11. Mutual submission as the fundamental principle of all relationships in the home and church (Romans 15:7).
12. Openness to the exercise of all biblical gifts of the Spirit without restriction on the basis of sex, status, age, education, or leadership position, (Acts 21:17) consistent with Scripture.
13. A commitment to evangelism and missions through the discipling of new converts by mature believers (Matthew 9:38).
14. The exercise of discipline and mutual admonition within the church according to New Testament principles (Matthew 18:15–18).
15. Maintaining a clear corporate witness and outspokenness against the evils of this present age (Galatians 5:20; Ephesians 5:5; Colossians 3:5).
16. A commitment to the kingdom of Christ that surpasses our allegiance to our nation, denomination, or any other system or ideology (Matthew 6:33).

What a supernatural, marvelous, awe-inspiring building and body is the Church of the Lord Jesus Christ when it exists and functions in the power of His Spirit, as He intended it should.
May we be that Church by His grace.

PART THREE

Where Do We Go From Here?

Finding a Living Church

You may agree about the sad condition of the church, but the vital question remains: if a church keeps on deteriorating and refuses to be made by God's design, where do we go from here? If you have a family you must do what is best for your children. And then the most important question to ask is, "What does *God* want me to do?"

It is not a pleasant job to look for another church because we all get socially attached where we are. But it is our duty, especially toward our children, when we discover that the church we attend is no longer a living church or a fellowship of true believers.

Do not be yoked together with unbelievers. For what do righteousness and wickedness have in common? ... For we are the temple of the living God ... therefore come out from among them and be separate, says the Lord.

(2 Corinthians 6:14–18)

The Bible says, *"Seek and you shall find,"* and how much more when we ask God to guide us in a matter as important as this. A living church can be large or small. Jesus even promised His presence where two or three are gathered in His name (Matthew 18:20). What does a living church look like?

A LIVING CHURCH

- It is mystical as it is built by God, controlled by the Spirit and not by men (Matthew 16:18).
- It is a plurality of leadership by spiritual elders and not by one man (Matthew 24:4, 5; Ephesians 5:6).
- It is a gathering primarily of believers and not of "seekers" (Hebrews 10:25).
- It is directed and purified by God's Spirit (John 16:13).
- It does not conform to worldly methods (Romans 12:1–2).
- It does not seek its own growth but establishes believers in the faith (Matthew 6:33; Philippians 2:21).
- It is divine in design and has gifted leadership (Matthew 16:18; Ephesians 4:11–13).
- It is compared, in structure, to a building (Ephesians 2:20), in functioning, to a body (Colossians 1:8), and in relationship, to a bride (2 Corinthians 11:2).

THE BENEFITS OF A LIVING CHURCH

- You will be encouraged to have a deeper personal relationship with God.

- You will grow in the grace and knowledge of our Lord.
- You will experience Christian love and fellowship with other believers.
- You will discover your gift and become a participant rather than a spectator in the growth of God's kingdom on earth.
- Your children will be encouraged to personally know and follow the Lord.
- You will become spiritually equipped and prepared for difficult times.

DIFFICULTIES FOR BOTH PASTORS AND LAY PEOPLE

Finding another church can be a hard choice for a layperson but consider how much harder this situation is for a pastor. Their career and security are both at stake. In spite of this, I have seen many great pastors managing their way through this, but for each one God's direction can be different.

If I were a pastor I would:

- Examine my current motives for being in ministry. If I had failed I would ask God to use me in bringing about a change.
- Want to be sure that my church was not man- but God-controlled with a team of trustworthy godly elders move in that direction.
- With their help, list the erroneous functions that perhaps have crept into the church and begin to pray and work towards a gradual change.
- Seek to remove all carnality in the church by inviting Jesus to be the head, directing all its actions.
- Strive to obey the biblical requirements for elders and leaders and gradually train gifted men for the work of the ministry.
- Practice expository preaching so that believers would begin to grow and become firm in their faith and fruitful in their walk.
- Encourage the whole church to be made up of small groups

who also would gather around the centrality of Jesus Christ, urging them to learn to bear one another's burden, experiencing renewed spiritual life through an atmosphere of openness and love.

- Endorse a program that would do with less staff, encourage voluntary lay ministries, gradually activating the body into ministry and reducing the financial overhead in the church.

AS A LAY PERSON YOU MUST MAKE A CHOICE

In general our options can be three-fold: flee, fight, or find.

FLEE

If your church has merged with the end-time church, no longer preaches the message of salvation (Hebrews 10:39), and no longer emphasizes the Christian walk, then we may very well ask, "What are we doing in an unproductive church?" (2 Corinthians 5:14–18). Or, *"Why are we seeking the living among the dead?"* (Luke 24:5).

To come out from among a Babylonian system is the only option the Bible gives us. This applies when you discover God's Word is no longer preached and personal salvation is being taken for granted. We, personally, have gone through such a situation, but then we saw dozens of people come to personal faith in Christ through meetings outside our church. The pastor and the elder board said, "Oh, you people are merely hypnotized, you were already Christians by our standards," however, we knew the truth.

Leaving that particular church was our only option. Later we were accused of "having taken the easy way out," but the opposite is true. Leaving the church of our upbringing was one of the hardest things we've ever had to do. Looking back, we have no regrets, and our family has been greatly blessed because we obeyed the Lord and found green pastures.

FIGHT

By fighting, I do not mean causing division within the church, but seeking to stop its decay through prayer. If you have to leave because there is no food for you or your children, go in peace, for this would be honoring to the Lord.

On the other hand, the Lord also placed us in churches that still had a good message, where the pastor was a real man of God, but the congregation had lost its first love and most of their young people had left. What a joy it was to help start a flame of new life in a group like that.

If you do not like what you hear or see in your church, it is your prophetic calling—not to do nothing—to blow a trumpet and do something trying to bring about change.

In one particular church, we started a lively weekly Bible class and many small house groups with the consent of the pastor. People began to open up, talk, confess their deadness, and pray. The atmosphere in the church began to change as we saw God at work! Our goal, first of all, was not to save the church but to help frustrated people in that system to come to life again. It was through this that the church was being blessed.

FIND

Finding a church that you know is somewhat formed by God's design and where He wants you to be is not an easy task. We live in an age of religious deception and ill-functioning churches that have turned off many people. We may never find a church where we are totally happy. Therefore we have to live with what we have and learn to be gracious as we pray this well-known prayer by Reinhold Niebuhr:

God, grant me the serenity to accept the things I cannot change. The courage to change the things I can and to know my limitations. Taking this sinful world as it is, not as I would have it. Trusting that You will make all things well, in Your time.

Often while being disappointed about a certain church, my prayer would include a tone of anger and frustration. Then God would answer back, "And how do you think I feel?" Dietrich Bonhoeffer, who struggled with a compromising church in Germany during Hitler's reign, in his excellent book *Life Together,* wrote about patience, love, and understanding and said: "If your love for the church is more than your love for truth then we have done the cause of Christ a disfavor."

In our life's journey, for seven years we also attended a church where the preaching was poor but the people were warm and the youth group was outstanding. It was for our children's sake we stayed, and as our children went through their teenage years they came out shining for the Lord. Seeing our children mature in the Lord and choose Christian life partners was worth staying in a church for their sake.

FINDING THE TREASURES

When we read about the end-times in the Bible, we read that false teachers will come. Their goal is money, but many will not see through that and will follow them. These deceivers will use Jesus as a drawing tool, but their deceitful emphasis is sensationalism with signs, wonders, prophecies, healing, and prosperity preaching. We are told not to follow them or have anything to do with them (Matthew 24:23–25).

Jesus, however, encouraged an entirely different approach when being in new surroundings. He told us to look for that "friendly person" (Matthew 10:12). The Bible tells us that a group is known by its people. How godly are the members in their walk? Do they live the Christian life or have the pleasures of this world gotten the best of them?

Finding a church within the church can become necessary for fellowship and your spiritual survival, even if it is a church that you merely tolerate on other matters. If there still is life in some of the people in the church but not in its structure, I would find like-minded Christians and, in small groups, begin to pray and build up each other. As believers, there is power when we come together for that purpose:

> *If my people, who are called by my name, will humble themselves and pray and seek my face and turn from their wicked ways, then will I hear from heaven.*
>
> (2 Chronicles 7:14)

Praying and meeting in small groups can become our best means for survival and the beginning of renewal. We must, however, know of what we should repent. Jesus promised where even two or three are gathered in his name, He is there to bless.

FINDING YOUR OWN

Have you ever considered who you are in Christ? You may have gifts you never realized you have. There might be dozens of others in your church as frustrated as you are. Many survive the storms of life and maintain spiritual growth by meeting with other believers in homes. Home groups, house groups, cell groups or survival groups, whatever you may call them, can be as much of a church as the church itself. Jesus never started a big church and, as already stated, He promised where two or three are gathered *in His Name* He would be there.

Even if you already go to church, home groups can supplement your diet and stimulate spiritual growth, as people learn to share and pray for each other. Home groups can mean healing for the wounded, encouragement for the distressed and salvation for those who seek. What tools do you need for this? You must come with an open mind, a servant heart, the right attitude, an open Bible, and faith in God. Try it; it works!

No, You Are Not Alone!

It was with this comment that I started these pages and with this I close. Have I been too harsh on the church? I'll let God be my judge, but I've made an attempt to express where I feel the church is missing the mark. You may not agree with all that has been written, but I encourage you to make use of the things you feel comfortable with and find biblically sound.

Obviously, I believe most churches have badly gone astray. Many are no longer preaching Christ's message but are abusing God's money and are grieving the Spirit. There are still some churches, however, that do a good job in proclaiming God's Word and maturing believers in the faith. I think of churches and TV programs led by men like Charles Stanley, Ravi Zacharias, David Jeremiah, John McArthur, Charles Price, and others.

These churches and programs are like beacons of light in a darkened world. Even these men would most likely agree that we are living in an age of rapid church decay and that many churches have already lost their purpose for existence.

Be not soon shaken in mind, or be troubled ... Let no man deceive you by any means: for that day shall not come, except there come a falling away first.
(2 Thessalonians 2:2–3, KJV)

Many who see this corruption in our churches have become discouraged and saddened. They are living in spiritual loneliness or isolation and are no longer gathering with other believers as we have been instructed to do.

Let us not give up meeting together, as some are in the habit of doing, but let us encourage one another—and all the more as you see the Day approaching.

(Hebrews 10:25)

Many feel like the prophet Elijah, who at times thought he was the only one being loyal to the Lord. It was then that the Lord revealed to him that there were seven thousand others just like him who had not bowed their knee to Baal (1 Kings 19).

So you are not alone in your struggle to find fellowship in order to remain faithful to the Lord. I have given several alternatives for your spiritual survival. Each person's situation is different, and what you do is a matter between you and God.

Our spiritual darkness will only get worse according to the prophetic Scriptures, but Jesus has clearly promised He will be with us to the end. At the same time we must not sit idly by but seek to minister to each other and remain useful to the Lord until He comes.

The Times of Elijah

See, I will send you the prophet Elijah before that great and dreadful day of the Lord comes. He will turn the hearts of the fathers to their children, and the hearts of the children to their fathers; or else I will come and strike the land with a curse (Malachi 4:5, 6).

Many people feel that there are enough evidences today to conclude that we are living in the end times. For this, among other things, they look at the restoration of Israel as a nation, the decay in the church, the signs in nature, political corruption, and the growing hatred towards Christianity.

Before that "Day of the Lord's" return and His vengeance upon the ungodly, we read in the very last verse of the Old Testament that God will send Elijah back to earth again. God will use once again this prophet of old to stand up against the same evil force he dealt with before.

THE TIMES

The times of Elijah were very much like the times we have today. Israel, much like the church, had turned its back on God-ordained ways of worship. Religion has become infiltrated with watered-down concepts of salvation, thus making room for other groups and beliefs. The god many now serve is a god after their own imagination—a god who only loves and who tolerates sin and immorality. It's like Israel's worship, which was no longer in obedience to the Spirit and truth but was the worship of Baal with loud noises and physical gestures. Yes, religious deception was the order of the day.

Elijah began to taunt them. "Shout louder!" he said ... "Maybe he is sleeping and must be awakened."(1 Kings 18:27).

A FALSE GOD AND FALSE PROPHETS

Serving a god after our own image is literally serving Baal. Like Israel of old, the end-times church is also strongly warned against Baal worship that is tolerated by religious leaders.

"I have heard what the prophets say who prophesy lies in my name. They say, 'I had a dream! I had a dream!' How long will this continue in the hearts of these lying prophets, who prophesy the delusions of their own minds? They think the dreams they tell one another will make my people forget my name, just as their fathers forgot my name through Baal worship. Let the prophet who has a dream tell his dream, but let the one who has my word speak it faithfully. For what has straw to do with grain?" declares the Lord. "Is not my word like fire," declares the Lord, "and like a hammer that breaks a rock in pieces?" (Jeremiah 23:25–29).

In the Old Testament, true prophets were men who were continually warning Israel against false religious leaders. Their condition was much like what we have today as the church is again infiltrated with false prophets who no longer proclaim God's message.

False prophets are those who claim to be serving God but are in reality catering to a man-made religious system. They are like Balaam who preached what the people wanted to hear (Revelation 2:14), claiming they had a word from God but in reality leading the people gradually into Baal worship.

Such people are in ministry for the wrong reasons and we are warned against preachers who are in it for profit and are deceiving and misleading the flock.

These men are blemishes at your love feasts, eating with you without the slightest qualm—shepherds who feed only themselves. They are clouds without rain, blown along by the wind; autumn trees, without fruit and uprooted—twice dead. They are wild waves of the sea, foaming up their shame; wandering stars, for whom blackest darkness has been reserved forever (Jude 12, 13).

ELIJAH, A TRUE PROPHET

In many ways Elijah was what pastors ought to be today. He was as human as we are when at times he was fearful and felt that he had to hide or run for his life. He did not come from a great notable family but basically came out of nowhere. But he became noticed when he was willing to stand up against the trend of his times and became a spokesman for God.

HE STOOD UP

Today we may sing "Stand up for Jesus" but do we actually dare to do that? Elijah was facing a mighty force—the king's wife, a powerful woman called Jezebel.

Today we are also facing an emerging religious system that is turning further and further away from God. They are neglecting Christ's intent for the church, which is maturing believers and reaching the unreached.

This end-times church movement is the man-made church that is not willing to repent from the errors of her ways. This movement is also called "Jezebel" and the Bible calls mixing falsehood with truth "committing adultery." We are not to tolerate such a system.

> *You tolerate that woman Jezebel, who calls herself a prophetess. By her teaching she misleads my servants into sexual immorality and the eating of food sacrificed to idols. I have given her time to repent of her immorality, but she is unwilling. So I will cast her on a bed of suffering, and I will make those who commit adultery with her suffer intensely, unless they repent of her ways* (Revelation 2:20–22).

HE THOUGHT HE STOOD ALONE

Even after his Mt. Carmel experience, Elijah, like Moses, felt totally inadequate for the task and God had to remind him:

> *Yet I reserve seven thousand in Israel—all whose knees have not bowed down to Baal and all whose mouths have not kissed him* (1 Kings 19:18).

We should also raise the battle cry today, challenging our pastors not to bow down to a wrong religious system but to be an Elijah or Daniel and to dare to stand up against the end-times tide.

HE RECOGNIZED GOD'S VOICE

If there is one thing we are lacking in most churches it is an elder leadership (pastors included) who have an ear to hear the voice of the Lord.

Elijah had to learn that God does not necessarily speak to us through an earthquake, a raging storm or in response to our raising our voices like the Baal worshippers. It was the still small voice that he realized to be God's voice and direction as it came to him. It is Jesus who wants to direct His church through people who can hear His voice and know His ways. This will make the church supernatural and not just another movement.

HE WAS WILLING TO ACCEPT REJECTION

Obedience to God's Word is always better than sacrifice. As believers in these end times, we will, if we do not go with the crowd, have to suffer a large amount of rejection even from those we thought were our fellow Christians.

Then you will be handed over to be persecuted and put to death, and you will be hated by all nations because of me. At that time many will turn away from the faith and will betray and hate each other, and many false prophets will appear and deceive many people (Matthew 24:9–11).

HE PREACHED THE MESSAGE OF THE LORD

Many preachers talk about the Bible but they don't give the message of the Bible. Many speak about revival and say that we need more of the Holy Spirit. This, however, is not what the Bible or Jesus tells us. Our Lord's message was about the authority God desires to have in our lives and in our churches. His message is still the same today, to all religious leaders as it was in Jesus' time. *"But unless you repent, you too will all perish"* (Luke 13:3).

Elijah's message was an urgent call to action:

How long will you waver between two opinions? If the Lord is God, follow Him, but if Baal is God, follow him (1 Kings 18:21).

HE WAS MIGHTY IN PRAYER

Have you ever considered what Jesus did before He fed the five thousand? We simply read that "He prayed." Of Elijah we read the same:

Elijah was a man just like us. He prayed earnestly that it would not rain, and it did not rain on the land for three and a half years. Again he prayed, and the heavens gave rain, and the earth produced its crops (James 5:17, 18).

The apostle James reminds us in this passage that the prayer of a righteous man is powerful and effective. A righteous person is a person who is pure in heart and motives before the Lord because: *"If I had cherished sin in my heart, the Lord would not have listened"* (Psalm 66:18).

May God help us to have the right motives when we pray and may we become clean vessels that He can use. We will see answers to prayer when we become a voice for restoration for Him and do not merely have a form of religion but have the power He wants to display through people who are in tune with Him.

HE WAS HONORED BY THE LORD

Jesus has a special reward waiting for them who have truly dared to stand up against the trend of their times.

My brothers, if one of you should wander from the truth and someone should bring him back, remember this: Whoever turns a sinner from the error of his way will save him from death and cover over a multitude of sins (James 5:19–20).

GOD'S CALL FOR PROPHETS

The apostle Paul emphasizes the role of the prophet as a most important function in the church. *"I would rather have you prophesy"* (1 Corinthians 14:5).

Could it be that today's church has come into being by human evolution instead of God's divine and intellectual design? Have we reached the stage where we merely preach Christianity or a Christian worldview and perspective but not Christ living within us? Are we living lives that are no longer filled with the indwelling and transforming power of Christ?

If you feel that this is where the church is today, I invite you to become an Elijah, a spokesperson for the Lord who will dare to stand up against the tide of our times *"If the trumpet does not sound a clear call, who will get ready for the battle?"* (1 Corinthians 14:8).

Ask God to empower you with His Spirit so that you may become like an Elijah, Daniel, or Joshua.

Be strong and courageous, because you will lead these people to inherit the land I swore to their forefathers to give them. Be strong and very courageous. Be careful to obey all the law my servant Moses gave you; do not turn from it to the right or to the left, that you may be successful wherever you go. Do not let this Book of the Law depart from your mouth; meditate on it day and night, so that you may be careful to do everything written in it. Then you will be prosperous and successful. Have I not commanded you? Be strong and courageous. Do not be terrified; do not be discouraged, for the Lord your God will be with you wherever you go (Joshua 1:6–9).

In this mission you will not be alone; millions are waiting for the sound of such a trumpet. The heavenly powers will be there to assist you and you will have a rich reward in eternity.

Personally, I have done my very best to write this manuscript and hereby must pass the torch on to others who will become agents of restoration, preparing, and healing the church in structure and vitality for the return of her Head.

If you, with me, are hoping to see a change come about in our churches, we invite you to help us in distributing this book to leaders who would appreciate to get this message. We have special rates available on bulk orders for those who want to become co-distributors. All royalties on this book will go to a Christian foundation.

Richard Oostra
E-mail: richardoostra@shaw.ca

Common Errors in the Church

Authority:

> Is the Church under direct control of Christ or some other authority?

Buildings:

> What has given us the right to return to temple structures?

Commercial:

> Hired employees and elaborate buildings have caused many churches to become commercial enterprises, forever in need of money.

Discipleship:

> It was Jesus' desire to build up believers into spiritual maturity for Him and not merely into easy believism.

Elders:

> The Bible gives us specific requirements for eldership. How well have we adhered to these in our churches?

False Prophets:

> Many churches are already infiltrated by tolerating and adding things the Bible clearly forbids (Revelation 22:18–19).

Godliness:

> The Bible speaks of believers as transformed people living holy lives. Why is holiness so little mentioned in our churches?

Humanism:

> We tolerate a very shallow faith in God with worldly lifestyles and values resulting into Bible illiteracy.

Individualism:
A practice of primarily seeking ourselves while the Bible so clearly speaks of self-denial and seeking God first.

Jargon:
A church may have all the religious terminology and rituals but if you do not see transformed lives, these are merely empty words.

Knowledge:
Spiritual knowledge without godly living is hypocritical and merely feeding the flesh and leading to spiritual misdirection.

Lawlessness:
Because of lack of love and the presence of God's Spirit, spiritual lawlessness has become very prevalent among believers.

Manipulation
Much manipulation done in the church today has deeply grieved the working of the Spirit and the loyalty of believers.

Nominalism:
Many bearing the name of Christian are only so in name. They believe the church can save them but have never received a new nature.

Overruled:
Having lost sight of the true meaning of godliness, many people have been given the wrong concept of salvation and now believe they will inherit eternal life by serving and being loyal to the church (Matthew 15:9).

Priesthood:
The priesthood of all believers is a term that has only been given lip-service to and is very seldom practiced today.

Questioning:
The authority of the Bible has taken second place to a system of theology made by men who ask "Has God said?"

Rejecting:
Rejecting biblical teachings on issues such as the structure of the church or separation from the world is the same as rejecting God's authority.

Salvation:
Salvation without repentance and change from within is not biblical salvation.

Teaching:
God's Word and His servants are meant to be our greatest teachers.

Unity:

> Jesus unites, but stressing secondary doctrines without tolerance to other insights divides and leads to legalism.

Victory:

> Victory in living the Christian life through the Spirit of God is attainable for all believers but no longer sought after by most believers.

Worldliness:

> Seeking to live at peace and loving friendship with the world is what the Bible calls enmity with Christ. Is this honoring God?

Xpect:

> When we seek to draw close to God, He will come close to us. When walking with God, we can expect great blessings from God.

You:

> Salvation is not a matter of belonging to a church but becoming related to God. You and each person are accountable for your own choice (Joshua 24:15).

Zero:

> Zero in on what you can restore and God will shed further light on your path. His Spirit will guide those who come to Him for help.

GOD'S PROMISE:

If my people, who are called by my name, will humble themselves and pray and seek my face and turn from their wicked ways, then will I hear from heaven and will forgive their sin and will heal their land (2 Chronicles 7:14).

HARSH WORDS FROM JESUS

It was about 95 AD when the apostle John, in exile on the island of Patmos, had a special revelation from the Lord. He was told what was going to happen to the churches in the years to come. The messages of Revelation 2 and 3 are severe warnings to the church. Although many religious leaders seek to explain them away, I have come to believe that they are especially for us who are living in the end-times because this is what the book of Revelation is all about. We are even told: *"Blessed is the one who reads the words of this prophecy, and blessed are those who hear it and take to heart what is written in it, because the time is near"* (Revelation 1:3).

167

LIVING IN LOVE

You have forsaken your first love (Revelation 2:4).

As important as the Great Commission is, of equal importance is Christ's Great Command that we, as Christians, should love each other.

Most Christians have memorized John 3:16, but very few can quote 1 John 3:16, which says we should love the Lord and other believers to the extent that we are willing to lay down our lives for each other. Instead, we live in an age of religious monastery-ism and self-sufficiency, and many pastors have become competitors over who has the largest church.

PERSECUTION READINESS

Do not be afraid of what you are to suffer ... Be faithful, even to the point of death, and I will give you the crown of life (Revelation 2:10).

For years the Western Church has soft-peddled the gospel. We have destroyed and nullified the true meaning of what it means to be a disciple, a Christ follower. Jesus forewarned us that as the world hated Him so they would hate us. But by taking away the cost of discipleship, we have created a society of Christian softies. Should we have to face any form of tribulation or persecution like our brothers in China we would not be able to stand and forgo the reward, the crown of life. "Standing firm to the end" is what Jesus expects of His followers.

DO NOT COMPROMISE

You have people there who hold to the teachings of Balaam ... You also have those who hold to the teaching of the Nicolaitans (Revelation 2:14, 15).

The Balaamites were those who served a god of their own design. How true that is today. We have brought the world into the church with our music as well as nullifying and soft-peddling the Word.

We no longer preach on the issue of sin, because we say, "God will forgive us all our sins; He is a God of Love." We no longer speak about the reality of hell nor about the Devil because we want to become "seeker-friendly" in our churches, and don't "wish to turn people and our youth away." We no longer have a biblical standard of eldership nor bring believers into discipleship. How low have we fallen in our churches!

TOLERATING FALSE PROPHETS

You tolerate that woman Jezebel, who calls herself a prophetess (Revelation 2:20).

As Christians we were meant to be overcomers and be able to stand up against wrong teachings and the ignoring of Scripture. When the Bible speaks of not offending the elderly, how do we dare walk over them with the new teachings, music, and other new methods we have in the church today?

Jesus has continually warned us that false teachers would come (Matthew 24:4, 11), but we have become so loyal to "our denomination" that we trust any pastor, even though he might be one of those false teachers who just does his job for money and no longer proclaims the truth of God's Word.

When we see no more conversions or meeting up to spiritual requirements for being a Christian, we should know we are in a church that has gone astray. The Bible forbids toleration and we must either blow the whistle or separate. The words of our Lord to Peter, *"Do you love these more than Me?"* also apply to us; otherwise we and our children will be falling out of God's grace (Revelation 18:4–5).

DEAD CHURCHES

I know your deeds, you have a reputation of being alive, but you are dead (Revelation 3:1).

It is very hard for one who has been for years in the church to admit that their church has grown cold and is spiritually dead. Jesus said that we will recognize deadness or life by the works they produce. When much of the work we see become social activities, catering to their own physical needs with little concern for the lost, then you will know what time it is.

Many ministers are merely career-seekers who have little knowledge of the Word and spiritual truth. They are Christian in name and, although loyal to the denomination, there is little loyalty to Christ or separation from the world.

For true believers in these churches the Bible has only one message: *"Wherefore come out from among them, and be ye separate"* (2 Corinthians 6:17).

Throughout the Bible we are encouraged to seek fellowship with other believers, but we are discouraged to be unequally yoked or seek the living among the dead.

THE REMNANT

You have kept my word and have not denied my name (Revelation 3:8).

Throughout Christian history there have always been segments that have lived in obedience to Christ's teachings. They have, at the risk of being persecuted, held fast to biblical truth as they read it in the Scriptures.

When Christ is in control in a church it will seek to obey His commandments, but when man is in control, corruption and decay will constantly enter in. This has been the cause of constant church splits and divisions in the Body of Christ.

Many carnal and nominal Christians do not like to talk about the end-times or the second coming of the Lord because they live in fear of Judgment Day. But in the book of Revelation Jesus says to the faithful: *"Since you have kept my commands ... I will also keep you from the hour of trial that is going to come upon the whole world to test those who live on the earth"* (Revelation 3:10).

Truly from Scripture we know that just before the final battle around Jerusalem with Satan's forces, God will send plagues upon the earth as a final warning for the people to repent (Revelation 6:17). But those who will be faithful unto the end (Matthew 24:13) will experience God's protection.

THE LUKEWARM

"Because you are lukewarm—neither hot nor cold—I am about to spit you out of my mouth" (Revelation 3:16).

Isn't it interesting that God's great invitation begins at John 3:16 and that His final warning to Christianity is Revelation 3:16?

Here we read of churches that have stored up great riches on earth and acquired great wealth, but the Bible calls these *"wretched, pitiful, poor, blind and naked"* (Revelation 3:17).

Would you want to belong to such a church? Earlier in the Bible we read that these churches have merely a form of godliness but not its transforming power. They refused the sound teachings of the Bible. Instead they developed a belief that suited their liking and catered to their system (2 Timothy 3:5, 4:3).

Christ's final warning to those leaders is that not everyone who says "Lord, Lord" is a believer and that He would spit them out of His mouth even though they claimed to have built great empires in His name.

His last words to them are: *"I never knew you. Away from me, you evildoers"* (Matthew 7: 23).

This passage in the Bible is a very severe warning to many who are in the wrong church and are not fully following Christ. There the most repeated phrase is: *"He, who has an ear, let him hear what the Spirit says to the churches"* (Revelation 2:17, 29; 3:6, 13, 22).

What is the Spirit saying? The message is either repent or perish: *"Come out of her, my people, so that you will not share in her sins, so that you will not receive any of her plagues"* (Revelation 18:4).

REGARD OR REGRET?

Together with the apostle John who warned those seven churches, I have also asked, why would a person in his latter years, after been deeply involved in different churches throughout his life, speak out against so many churches of today? A dear friend even warned me that if I would publish this manuscript I would be highly criticized, and my name would be mud, but this risk I am willing to take.

Most people do not want to speak up for the truth, but would rather be "politically correct" and by being silent keep the peace.

Yet, when we know something is wrong, is it right to remain silent? Israel of old was continually subjected to warnings from God through many prophets. Today, however, we have eliminated most ministries of the Spirit, including the role of the prophets.

It would be much easier to keep silent on the things I have written about and make myself less vulnerable, but that would be practicing the sin of omission. Speaking up against the church is like touching so many people's "golden calf," which also Israel began to worship while Moses was on the mountain.

Even as David wrote: *"When I kept silent, my bones wasted away"* (Psalm 32:3).

A brother of Jesus stated: *"My brothers, if one of you should wander from the truth and someone should bring him back,"* (James 5:19).

Yes, the ministry of correction is not an easy one, because many will furiously defend their church. But if we truly love each other, we must be willing to offer and accept correction; otherwise we become participants in wrongdoings. *"Let no one deceive you with empty words, for because of such things God's wrath comes on those who are disobedient. Therefore do not be partners with them"* (Ephesians 5:6, 7).

The Pharisees in Jesus' times refused to accept all the corrections Jesus offered them. As a matter of fact they even tried to find fault with the people Jesus healed because He did it on the Sabbath. By this they were legalistically trying to protect their ill-functioning religious system.

Yes, you will no doubt find loopholes in what I have written. I have spoken up because I care for the church, but not at the expense of refusing to speak up for the truth I see in Scripture.

Starting with the Church of Rome, the church of today is based on a religious system that has continued to follow her pattern of manipulation and enforcement of half-truths that have turned so many people away from following Christ.

When the Israelites or the people of Nineveh came to repentance, they admitted and confessed their sins. They would call for a solemn assembly, list their sins and pray for forgiveness as they called upon the Lord. Today, we only pray for revival, but without confession and repentance of sin there will be no restoration.

As spelled out already, the sins of the Church are as long as the alphabet. Some of these are:

- Having become a commercialized religion making careerism out of ministry.
- Having changed the role of the pastor-shepherd into a CEO of an organization and in doing so having established a system of papal hierarchy.
- Having ignored the Kingship of Christ by letting people control the church, thus making the church a kingdom unto itself.
- Having restored the Old Testament priesthood with clergy as priest and temples in which we gather, thus making many think that being a Christian is belonging to a church.
- Having institutionalized the church to the extent that believers are no longer a kingdom of priests, but hearers only, and are no longer equipping each other for ministry.
- Having added to the Bible by making additional creeds and confessions. In doing so we have established many denominations and no longer have need of the Holy Spirit to teach and guide us into all truths, because ours is "the only right interpretation of the Bible."
- Having rejected the supernatural control of the Spirit, we are now producing merely an imitation form of godliness. We are no longer experiencing the power the church could have.

But has God forsaken His Church? Most certainly not! All true believers belong to the universal Church of God. In the same way God still loves

Israel and will restore her, so He will restore the church.

The message of the prophet Isaiah still stands for today: *"Though your sins are like scarlet, they shall be as white as snow; though they are red as crimson, they shall be like wool"* (Isaiah 1:18).

This, however, is based upon a church coming together to the Lord. Those who will continue to go on in the errors of their ways or prefer to live in spiritual darkness must remember that God's Spirit will not forever strive with them. The time for judgment is drawing nigh.

Jesus and the prophets, throughout the Bible, have warned us of end-time events that are soon to come. We, who have the Scriptures, are without an excuse for not having knowledge of what lies ahead.

Have we prepared ourselves and our families for the end-time purification and persecution Jesus told us to be prepared for before His return? Or have we become totally blinded by men's philosophies and doing what Jesus warned us about? *"You nullify the word of God for the sake of your tradition"* (Matthew 15:6).

The reason for this writing is that those belonging to various religious institutions might know the saying "buyer beware." The Bible challenges those living in the end-times to let those who are holy become more holy yet, because what is wicked will become more wicked yet (Daniel 12:10; Revelation 22:11).

May the reader understand the concern of the writer and the patience and love of the heavenly Father. May this cause us to come to repentance toward God. Then, with the apostle, we can say: *"Even if I caused you sorrow by my letter, I do not regret it ... Godly sorrow brings repentance that leads to salvation and leaves no regret"* (2 Corinthians 7:8, 10).

The Seduction of Our Churches

They received the message with great eagerness and examined the Scriptures (Act 17:11).

Believers who have become frustrated in their churches often have the same question the disciples had, "What will be the sign of the end times?"

The answer for them is found in 1 Peter 5:8. Here we read that we must be on our guard for Satan is going around like a roaring lion and no doubt luring pastors by giving them a strong desire for church growth. He is causing them to make many unbiblical changes that will eventually lead to the destruction of the church.

DECEPTION USED

Again in 1 Peter 5:1–4, leaders are warned not to become CEOs or to be striving for power or be greedy for money or position, but to remain shepherds to the flock by being examples of godliness.

In the latter days, Jesus says that even children will stand up against their parents (Matthew 10:21) much like it was in the days of Israel's decay.

The young will rise up against the old ... Youths oppress my people, women rule over them. O my people, your guides lead you astray; they turn you from the path (Isaiah 3:5, 12).

DECAY PREDICTED

The Bible teaches us in 1 Peter 4:17 that in the end times the decay will begin at the house of God. Jesus also raised the question: *"When the Son of Man comes, will he find faith on the earth?"* (Luke 18:8).

Throughout the Bible it has been predicted that before Christ's return sinful men will have turned the truth of God's Word into a lie and the church will experience an age of apathy (Matthew 24:4–13; 2 Peter 3:3–4).

As an act of desperation, many pastors are not asking "Where have we gone wrong?" but are now turning to the "church growth movement." The answer received from these sources is to make the service and the message attractive to the youth and the un-churched. They are told to forget about the subject of sin and the ugliness of the cross. Instead, they should preach the love of God and the benefits of being a Christian. Today, God has become everyone's friend, Jesus is our buddy, and the Holy Spirit is a source of entertainment. Truly, the church has become an attraction, but the fear of the Lord is no longer in them (Psalm 36:1).

DESERTION OF TRUTH

If there is one sin we commit in today's church, it is lowering Christ's standard of salvation. We have been only proclaiming a gospel of grace and no longer requiring a life of obedience to the Lord. The church, for example, was meant to be a gathering of believers but now we are seeking to draw and please the unbeliever. The church was meant to be governed by elders who knew the Word, who met up to biblical requirements, and could lead the flock. Pastors now seek to draw the younger generation as elders who are in agreement with their new ideals.

The church was meant to mature its flock into disciples—those who have matured and walk in obedience of the faith. Today, we offend the elderly with our music, we tolerate divorce and remarriage, women in leadership, and worldly conformity. Basically, everyone can do what is right in their own eyes. But the Bible still tells us: *"Now that you have purified yourselves by obeying the truth so that you have sincere love for your brothers, love one another deeply, from the heart"* (1 Peter 1:22).

DEVALUATING THE GOSPEL

Most pastors are obsessed to make the church look "cool." The new approach to accomplish this is a contextualizing of Christianity into our present culture. It is conforming to the spirit of the times. We are adopting worldly marketing methods. For this we are using contemporary music placed in Christian settings.

The question, "What does the Lord say?" has been replaced with, "What does it take to draw the youth and bring in a crowd?" It is no longer sound doctrine or biblical correctness that matters. They prioritize what outsiders like to hear. This is so sad because the Bible clearly teaches us not to conform to this world and that the ways and methods of this world are not God's ways of building his church (Zechariah 4:6). Even our worship can not be acceptable to the Lord if it is offensive and causing grief and division in the body (Matthew 5:23).

DELUSION FORETOLD

They perish because they refused to love the truth and so be saved. For this reason God sends them a powerful delusion so that they will believe the lie (2 Thessalonians 2:10, 11).

Of Israel we read that God gave them their request but sent leanness to their soul. Yes, it is a serious matter once we start polluting God's people and ignore the truth of His Word. In this age of apostasy we have ignored the feelings of the elderly and the teachings of the Bible. We are preaching faith without obedience, and the Bible calls this "believing in vain." We are asking the elderly for tolerance and endurance, claiming what is being done is for the good of the church while we are on a speedway to utter destruction.

If we as parents had catered to our children like the church does today, would they have ever turned out as believers? The Bible so clearly teaches us not to remove the landmark the elders have set (Proverbs 23:10) or:

Don't let others spoil your faith and joy with their philosophies, their wrong and shallow answers build on men's thoughts and ideas instead of what Christ has said (Colossians 2:8 TLB).

DISCARDING CHRIST'S TEACHINGS

The church belongs to Christ and it is upon Christ's teachings we must build the church. It cannot be built upon human philosophy or conforming to the ways and methods of this world. Again the Bible teaches us if we want to rescue anything by human scheming we will eventually lose it (Mark 8:35).

Yet, many pastors, by trying to save the church and thinking to help the Lord with this, are "touching the ark" (1 Chronicles 13:9). They merely present the attractiveness and human benefits of the gospel. Besides this, they are allowing the youth to bring rock 'n' roll music into the church. Listen to what the Lord of the church has to say:

If anyone is ashamed of me and my words in this adulterous and sinful generation, the Son of Man will be ashamed of him when he comes in his Father's glory with the holy angels (Mark 8:38).

DAMAGING RESULTS

The smooth response that is given to those who feel disturbed about what is happening in the church is "be tolerant." They are told all will be well eventually as long as they are patient. This theory has become Satan's weapon, destroying the church from within. The Bible teaches: *"There is a way that seems right to a man, but in the end it leads to death"* (Proverbs 14:12).

How dare we and our pastors and elders remain silent when we know that we are grieving the Holy Spirit with the music we use? We are offending the elderly; causing many to leave; discouraging many to bring in new people; dividing and destroying the church.

The Bible speaks of harmony and love when it says: *"I will praise God's name in song and glorify him with thanksgiving. This will please the LORD"* (Psalm 69:30, 31).

The Bible clearly teaches us not to be partakers or even tolerate (Revelation 2:2, 20) these evil deeds of those who no longer hold to God's Word. We are not to trample upon God's requirements for holiness, reverence, and respect in God's house, but to seek separation from the world.

DIRECTED TO ACTION

God's warning to pastors in the Old Testament also applies to us:

"Woe to the shepherds who are destroying and scattering the sheep of my pasture!" declares the Lord. Therefore this is what the Lord, the God of Israel, says to the shepherds who tend my people: "Because you have scattered my flock and driven them away and have not bestowed care on them, I will bestow punishment on you for the evil you have done" (Jeremiah 23:1, 2).

In case you think this to be an isolated passage, I invite you to turn to Ezekiel 34:2 or Zechariah 11:17. Even in Matthew 23, Jesus speaks very similarly to the false pastors in his day. Then in 1 Corinthians 9:16 the apostle Paul warns us of the woes that will come to them who do not in purity proclaim Christ's gospel.

178

The Bible speaks of the sins of commission as well as omission. The church was meant to be a place of learning and spiritual growth for the believer. So what are we to do if the service becomes a noisy event, when we hear no more messages from God? What are we to do when everything goes and there are no more absolutes such as a narrow way and a broad way, a heaven and a hell, a kingdom of light and a kingdom of darkness?

This is what the Bible says:

Do not share in the sins of others. Keep yourself pure (1 Timothy 5:22).

Let no one deceive you with empty words, for because of such things God's wrath comes on those who are disobedient. Therefore do not be partners with them (Ephesians 5:6, 7).

Come out of her, my people, so that you will not share in her sins, so that you will not receive any of her plagues; for her sins are piled up to heaven, and God has remembered her crimes (Revelation 18:4,5).

May God help us not to be loyal to a dying church but to His Word.

Why No Prophecy?

The Bible is (for twenty five percent of its content) a book of prophecy. Yet in our churches today we seldom hear a message relating to Bible prophecy or of the keeping of God's commandments. As a result, most Christians are unaware of what lies ahead or what the Lord requires of them in order to live the Christian life. Spiritually we are floating down the river not knowing the signs of what lies ahead of us. Such is the condition of the church today.

> *As it was in the days of Noah, so it will be at the coming of the Son of man ... people were eating and drinking, marrying and giving in marriage, up to the day Noah entered the ark; and they knew nothing about what would happen until the flood came and took them all away* (Matthew 24:37–39).

The Second Coming of Christ will be the most important event to come and yet even in the church today we are filled with scoffers who say *"Where is this 'coming' he promised?"* (2 Peter 3:4).

A lady I know had asked several pastors why they no longer preach about the return of Jesus to this earth. These are the answers she received:

"End-times doctrines are too controversial"

"Many have sensationalized this topic, that is why I do not touch it."

"I don't know where I stand on that subject."

"I am a pan-tribulationist—it will all pan out in the end. Ha! Ha!"

"Why worry? We will be raptured anyway."

Yet the Second Coming of Christ is predicted in each of the four gospels, in the book of Acts, and in the epistles of Paul, James, Peter and John. Jesus' return and the end time events are the focal points of the entire book of Revelation. We are challenged to read and come to understand this book above any other book in the Bible.

Still most pastors remain silent on this subject because they themselves do not embrace this hope-giving, purifying truth about Christ's return. Others think it not to be "cool" to preach on a subject that may disturb the people.

Jesus gave many predictions and signs for us to be aware of prior to His coming. Who are we to ignore these? He even said: "*Watch ye therefore, and pray always, that ye may be accounted worthy to escape all these things that shall come to pass,*" (Luke 21:36 KJV).

Have we come to a time of a spiritual famine because our shepherds no longer feed the flock? Are they "No longer taking heed to declare us the whole counsel of God" (Acts 20:21), but only interested in feeding themselves? (Ezekiel 34:3).

People need to be taught what the Bible tells us about the signs Jesus gave us predicting the end-times; about the Antichrist who will soon appear with signs and wonders seeking to deceive, if it were possible, the very elect; about the hatred towards Christianity and tribulations to come of which Jesus said "Unless those days were shortened, no flesh would be saved" (Matthew 24:22, NKJV).

What do we know about the signs Jesus told us to be aware of in nature, the universe, and in the church? Do not the political happenings today relate to many yet-to-be-fulfilled prophecies that are no longer mentioned in our pulpits? Do we not see global events taking place that move toward a world government and a unified religious system that merely will have a form of godliness? (2 Timothy 3:5). Yes, many people feel that something is about to happen but:

1. They are not taught or instructed regarding end-time events.
2. They know the Bible is God's book but they do not know what it says.
3. They know things are coming to an end but are careless, thinking God will take care of them.

If we would only begin to study Matthew 24 (with Jesus' predictions), the book of Daniel, and the revelations given us by Paul, Peter, and John on these things, we would begin to receive, through the Spirit's guidance, great insights into the timing and God's plan for the future.

Just remember the Bible is God's handbook for:

Basic **I**nstructions **B**efore **L**eaving **E**arth.

Too many, however, only want to believe what our churches teach on a subject. Even if that is not much, they will never look for other insights, preferring to remain ignorant and blind.

It is so interesting to note that Jesus, after He spoke about the end-times in Matthew 24, continues on in Matthew 25 by giving us the parable of the Ten Virgins. Have you ever thought of relating this parable to our preparedness for the end-times?

These bridesmaids were all waiting for the arrival of the bridegroom just as believers should be living in anticipation of Christ's return today. Five were well-prepared, in case His return might be later than they had hoped for. The others were not. These were not prepared for any tribulation or, as Jesus said, "enduring to the end." They ran out of oil. Oil here speaks of a spiritual readiness. They were ill or uninformed of what they might have to endure in the end-times. They were not "in the know" regarding the signs to look for preceding Christ's return. They had fallen asleep sitting in a church pew, being told that all was well while it was not. They were told that Christ's coming could be another thousand years away! They had not taken heed of Christ's warnings against being influenced by false teachers even if they could perform signs and miracles. They had not lived in separation from the world but had become conformed to the things in their church and their pastors willful ignorance toward the warnings of Jesus and the prophesies in the Bible.

Even so, when you see these things happening, you know that the kingdom of God is near (Luke 21:31).

Becoming an Agent for Change

ROMANS 12

In the book of Romans we, as Christians, are being challenged to live a life in full commitment and obedience to God, even in the way we run our churches. Having seen how far the Church is off track, many will ask, "Is there any hope for change?"

Yes, everything is possible for those who are willing to make a new commitment. The apostle Paul, who was perhaps the greatest apostle, shares with us in Romans 12 what it will take to become an agent for change.

BE SURRENDERED TO GOD

Offer your bodies as living sacrifices to God (vs.1).

The trouble in the church, as one speaker recently said, is that much of Christendom runs sixteen miles wide but only a quarter of an inch deep. The Bible also tells us that when Jesus was on earth "many believed in Him," but that same crowd would shout a short time later "Crucify Him," because they did not want Jesus to reign over them.

Many claim to know Jesus whether it is through baptism, intellectually believing, or church membership, but the most crucial question is, "Does Jesus know them as being His?"

The apostle Paul is our strongest example of a man who was fully committed to the Lord. What was his secret?

"... so that I might live for God. I have been crucified with Christ and I no longer live, but Christ lives in me" (Galatians 2:19–20).

It is when we surrender ourselves to Jesus and let Him live His life through our bodies that we become agents for change. Jesus said: *"I am the vine; you are the branches. If a man remains in me and I in him, he will bear much fruit"* (John 15:5).

Have you ever in full surrender prayed: *"Lord, all that I am and have, my career, ministry, sphere of influence, I place it all to your service and disposal"*?

When I had my business I placed this, as it were, on the altar many times, and it was a joy to see the ways God used it!

SEPARATED FROM THE WORLD

Do not be conformed to this world, but be transformed (vs. 2).

In many cases today we do not see much difference in appearance, lifestyle, or attitudes between a person of the world or a Christian. Even in our churches we have many worldly and materialistic tendencies because it is often run by people who are interested in what is in it for them. This leaves a very materialistic impression upon those attending.

How we do things indicates the choice as to whether or not we want to be a Christ- follower. The surrendered ministry or person who wants to be used by God as an agent for change must want to operate by God's design and for His purposes.

The Bible tells us that friendship or conformity to this world is basically enmity against God, but the apostle tells us:

"Love not the world or anything of this world. If anyone loves the world, the love of the Father is not in him" (1 John 2:15).

What the world has to offer is all based on lust such as position, power, or possessions, and these are often worked out as things, sex, or sensuality. The Bible, however, warns us that these things will someday become worthless, but he who does the will of God will find lasting joy and fruitfulness that will continue into eternity.

SOBER IN SELF-PERSPECTIVE

Do not think of yourself more highly that you ought (vs. 3-8).

Becoming an agent for change does not lie in creating a great image of one's organization but in having the Spirit of God working through it.

Today, on the church page, we see churches advertising themselves as being the greatest, the friendliest, or the most exclusive church, while at the same time the Bible teaches:

"Do nothing out of selfish ambition or vain conceit, but in humility consider others better than yourself" (Philippians 2:3).

As Christian groups we all have different ministries. We therefore do not have to compete with each other but serve in unity and humility. Those who may feel inadequate toward becoming an agent for change must learn to say with the apostle:

"I can do all things through Christ, who gives me the strength" (Philippians 4:13).

SERVING IN LOVE

Be devoted to one another in brotherly love (vs. 10).

Most Christian leaders are familiar with John 3:16 which speaks of God's supernatural love, but what about 1 John 3:16? Here we read that if we have fully surrendered ourselves to Him, He will enable us to have a sacrificial love for others.

" Jesus Christ laid down his life for us. And we ought to lay down our lives for our brothers."

This kind of love is divine love that does not seek self-status or prestige but causes one to want to be a doer of the will of God. It is an obedience, if need to be, unto death, and a wholehearted caring for the body of believers, even by taking a risk toward change.

SUPERNATURALLY RESPONDING TO OPPOSITION

Bless those who oppose you and do not resent (vss. 12–14).

In wanting to become an agent for change we must realize that for every amount of action, we will find an even greater amount of reaction.

By no longer wanting to fit into the religious pattern of His day, Jesus caused a tremendous amount of opposition. So what can we expect if we dare to speak up against a religious system that is no longer formed by Christ's design? Jesus said that those who opposed Him will also oppose us. It was the religious people of His day who said, "We will not have this man rule over us," because Jesus threatened the very being of their livelihood and pride.

Our response to those who resent or oppose us should be like that of a dead man. In order to do this we must be unresponsive because of having died with Christ.

"I have been crucified with Christ and I no longer live but Christ lives in me" (Galatians 2:20). Or as Jesus said it: *"Unless a kernel of wheat falls to the ground and dies ... it produces many seeds"* (John 12:24).

Someone has said that total commitment is the channel through which God's best and biggest blessings flow. Offering ourselves in obedience to God's grace, Christ's example and the Spirit's enablement should make us willing to die to our own interests and becoming an agent for change to the glory of God.

Many have sacrificially taken such a stand before, are you willing to follow?

Church on the Rock

Church on the Rock is not for those who are satisfied with their church, but for the disillusioned and the confused.

Church on the Rock is about what Jesus intended His church to be of which He said, "I will build my church" (Matt 16:18).

Church on the Rock is about present day church decay and the root cause of it.

Church on the Rock reminds us that Christ instructed us to be Kingdom builders and not church makers.

Church on the Rock presents the fact that our reversal of the Kingdom mandate to church promotion was predicted in the Bible (Matt 11:12 KJV).

Church on the Rock refers to Peter's confession (Matt 16:18) which ought to be the Rock on which every church is build.

Church on the Rock encourages us not to build on earthly rocks such as dogmas, creeds and other writings.

Church on the Rock reminds us that the Headship of Christ is only experienced when His directive voice is heard by godly elders (John 10:3,16,27).

Church on the Rock speaks of the Church that is experiencing Christ's presence because if we do not gather with Him we will continually be divided (Matt 12:30).

Church on the Rock warns of churches where no conversions are seen and people are not urged to enter by the narrow gate (Matt 7:13,14).

Church on the Rock reminds us that we are living in the age of church decay and that we must be aware of false teachings in order not to be deceived (I Pet 4:17).

Church on the Rock is a book with sobering facts so that sincere believers will remain alert and keep themselves pure from worldly trends.

Church on the Rock invites true believers to action, daring to take a stand against corruption and decay.

INDEX